PRAISE FOR

How to Counsel a Couple in Six Sessions or Less

Having Norm Wright's marriage counseling information in one, easy-to-read, concise book will be very useful. The questionnaire definitely cuts to the chase and will be helpful for me (or a counselor on our staff) to quickly get to the heart of the matter. I really do like that!

STEVE ABRAHAM
PASTOR, NEW LIFE CHURCH

I enjoyed reading *How to Counsel a Couple in Six Sessions or Less*. Dr. H. Norman Wright gives a practical resource to clergy and counselors who provide marriage counseling. This book will better equip pastors to help couples remain more happily married. Thank you, Dr. Wright, for the skills and strategies presented in this book—they will help me to be a better clergy counselor!

DR. DANIEL BORG
PASTOR, BETHANY BAPTIST CHURCH

As you look at this book's title, you might say to yourself, "Sure, you can counsel a couple in six sessions or less, but will it do any good? Can meaningful change take place that quickly?" After providing literally thousands of hours of marital counseling over the past 30 years, my answer is a resounding yes! Research on treatment outcome consistently shows that quality short-term treatment can be as effective as long-term therapy. A 12-year study published by a nationally known psychiatric institute showed that clients receiving brief therapy profited as much from that approach as those who received long-term treatment. This book will help you help couples by providing meaningful short-term solutions that can bear long-term benefits.

DR. GARY OLIVER, TH.M., PH.D.
EXECUTIVE DIRECTOR, THE CENTER FOR MARRIAGE AND FAMILY STUDIES
PROFESSOR OF PSYCHOLOGY AND PRACTICAL THEOLOGY,
JOHN BROWN UNIVERSITY
DEVELOPER, GROWTH-FOCUSED BRIEF THERAPY
SENIOR AUTHOR, *PROMOTING CHANGE THROUGH BRIEF THERAPY
IN CHRISTIAN COUNSELING*

Norm Wright has done it again! Immensely practical. Outcome oriented. And biblically grounded. *How to Counsel a Couple in Six Sessions or Less* is urgently needed and long overdue. Finally, we get a good look at exactly how Norm has been so successful with helping so many couples. This valuable book and diagnostic tool should be in the office of every pastor and counselor. We can't recommend it enough!

DRS. LES AND LESLIE PARROTT
SEATTLE PACIFIC UNIVERSITY
AUTHORS, *SAVING YOUR MARRIAGE BEFORE IT STARTS*

How to Counsel a Couple in 6 SESSIONS or Less

Dr. H. Norman Wright

Regal

From Gospel Light
Ventura, California, U.S.A.

Published by Regal Books
From Gospel Light
Ventura, California, U.S.A.
Printed in the U.S.A.

Cover and interior design by Robert Williams
Edited by Amy Simpson

Library of Congress Cataloging-in-Publication Data

Wright, H. Norman.
      How to counsel a couple in six sessions or less / H. Norman Wright.
            p.   cm.
Includes bibliographical references.
      ISBN 0-8307-3068-0 (trade paper)
      1.   Marriage counseling. 2.   Pastoral counseling. I. Title.
      BV4012.27 .W74 2002
      259' .14—dc21   2002008100

3   4   5   6   7   8   9   10   11   12   13   14   15   /   09   08

Rights for publishing this book in other languages are contracted by Gospel Light Worldwide, the international nonprofit ministry of Gospel Light. Gospel Light Worldwide also provides publishing and technical assistance to international publishers dedicated to producing Sunday School and Vacation Bible School curricula and books in the languages of the world. For additional information, visit www.gospellightworldwide.org; write to Gospel Light Worldwide, P.O. Box 3875, Ventura, CA 93006; or send an e-mail to info@gospellightworldwide.org.

CONTENTS

Chapter 1

WHEN A COUPLE SEEKS YOUR HELP

"Pastor, can you help us? Our marriage is falling apart.
　　You're our last hope."
"Pastor, you've got to straighten out my wife's thinking.
　　It's affecting our marriage!"
"Pastor, what do I do? It's his third affair."

These familiar words often come from a desperate phone call. You are asked to do the impossible and repair years of destruction. Can you help them? Can you do anything? And can you devote the time that's needed to assist them? Through this resource, it is my hope to provide you with answers to these questions and more, *paying particular attention to how you can counsel a couple effectively by sticking to a plan where you will evaluate a couple and then determine their needs in six sessions or less.*

EXPECTATIONS

Remember that you will not help every couple who comes to you. It would be dangerous to use statistics of how many couples still divorce as criteria for counseling success. With this in mind, it is critical that you know your own expectations as couples seek your assistance so that one day you don't blame yourself for a failed marriage.

The reasons behind couples seeking help vary greatly. One couple might come to see you as a token effort to show that they have tried to save their marriage, but their hearts aren't in it and likely they have already decided to divorce. On the other hand, another couple might not benefit from counseling because you just don't connect with them. This is okay. You won't be able to work well with everyone who comes to see you. Some will come wanting you to take sides and when you don't, they will tune out even the most helpful suggestions. Others will resist only because they don't like your recommendation to a problem, while some are unwilling to change no matter how skilled you are. But always remember that it is important to come to grips with the fact that you are neither responsible for their past, nor can you fix their relationship for them. You cannot force them to do anything. In all likelihood, you will not have the time that is needed to help some couples sort through their issues in order to turn their marriages around.[1]

I like what DeLoss and Ruby Friesen suggest concerning how your own values will affect what you do, as well as what you can expect from yourself.

It's not possible or desirable to completely separate your values from the situation. The counselor, however, may reveal his or her values without imposing those values on the counselee. For example, we will share, if appropriate, our belief (value) that many more couples could make their marriages work if they were more committed to doing so. Not all of our couples share this belief.[2]

The Friesens go on to list some realistic expectations for the counselor:

- You may be able to set achievable goals by helping to identify the real issues involved and whose issues they are.
- You may be able to help with behavior changes that will work toward achieving the goals of the couple.
- You may be able to help sort out various options and the consequences of choosing or not choosing these options.
- You can work with the couple as a team to try to find solutions.
- You can help the couple identify strengths and how they might use their strengths in a particular situation.
- You can help individuals develop more control over their own destinies (by taking responsibility for one's own happiness, greater happiness in the marriage may follow).
- You may be able to help the couple accept past events; they can learn that the past does not always have to forecast the future.
- You may be able to act as a stabilizing force when the couple has lost hope.[3]

However, the greater the severity of the problems, the more likely a couple's help will be limited. Dr. Everett Worthington suggests the following:

Couples with severe problems usually require more sessions and usually improve less than couples with less severe difficulties. But what is a severe difficulty?[4]

Worthington expands on his "What is a severe difficulty" question with at least eight important predictors of poor counseling outcome, which, based on my own experiences, almost always result from what some counselors consider "severe difficulties." It is my conclusion that the more difficulties a couple experiences, the less success the counselor will have. Keep these in mind when evaluating a couple, and you could save yourself time, energy and frustration.

1. An ongoing affair that one spouse refuses to terminate.
2. One or both spouses use overt threats of divorce and a lawyer has been contacted.
3. Presence of severe personal problems such as chronic depression or alcoholism.
4. Both spouses are non-Christians or involved only on the fringes of the organized church. Or if one spouse is bitterly opposed to Christianity and the other is actively involved in it, the effect is similarly pessimistic, though the couple will tend to have different problems.
5. Lack of intimacy and pleasantness in the couple's interaction. This is different from the presence of hostility and negative behavior.
6. Severe patterns of conflict that are harmful, overlearned, well rehearsed, deeply disturbing and demoralizing. Conflict involves power struggles that are well entrenched. During conflict, the couple attacks each

other personally and disparages the worth of the relationship.

7. Continual focus on the problems with the relationship and with the spouse. If the couple returns to the deficiencies in the relationship and the spouse, even when the counselor persistently induces them to discuss other topics, the relationship will require more effort than if the couple cooperates with the counselor.

8. Involvement of "helpers" who encourage individual spouses to protect themselves in the relationship. In-laws tend to play this role. One can understand their proclivity to protect their offspring through advice and sometimes interference, but their intervention forces the marriage apart. Other parties that can become over-involved in marriage struggles and make success less likely are: individual counselors, pastors, influential friends and siblings.[5]

Can you see why certain issues would make it difficult to help turn a marriage around?

PRECOUNSELING

How would you begin your first session with a couple? Have you ever considered the possibility of getting the couple to work out problems before they see you? Here is a verbatim quote from the book *Promoting Change Through Brief Therapy in Christian Counseling*, which illustrates what you can suggest to a couple before the counseling sessions begin.

Susan: My husband and I need some help with our marriage.

Counselor: How are you hoping I might be able to help you?

Susan: Well, we don't communicate very well, and we argue more than I like. I've wanted to get some counseling for a long time, and Jim finally said he'd be willing to come.

Counselor: Susan, there are two important things you and Jim can do before our first session. Doing these two things will help you get much more benefit from our time together. The first one is (if after) our first session we agree to work together, what would have to happen for you to know that the counseling had made a positive difference in your marriage relationship? Another way of looking at this is to ask yourself, "When will we know that we no longer need to come in for counseling?" Do you think you and Jim can do that?

Susan: Sure. What's the second thing?

Counselor: Well, the second task is easier than the first. In the past several years, I've had many couples tell me that they experienced some small improvements between the time they made the phone call and their first session. Between now and your first appointment, I'd like you and Jim to notice any positive or pleasant things that happen in your relationship. You may want to write them down and bring the lists with you, even if the lists only have one thing.

Susan goes home and tells her husband, Jim, the counselor's two points they need to focus on before their first session. Here is a dialogue of the first session.

Counselor: When we talked on the phone, I asked you to think about what would need to happen for you to know that our work together was helpful. Jim, what did you come up with?

Jim: Well, one of the main things is that we wouldn't argue so much. Sometimes I come home from work, and as soon as I walk in the door, I feel attacked. It feels as if she can't wait to pounce on me.

Susan (With a disgusted look and a sarcastic tone of voice.): If you'd come home when you say you would, maybe you wouldn't feel so attacked. I'm sick and tired of working hard to have dinner ready, getting the kids to the table and then having you waltz in at least one hour late. And you don't even call to say you'll be late.

Counselor: Susan, so one of the ways you would know whether Jim was really committed to working on improving your marriage is if he came home when he said he would?

Susan: Yes, that would be a great start.

Counselor: Jim, how realistic is that?

Jim: I guess I could do that. I mean, I'm on time for appointments at work. But I don't know if I can be on time every night.

Counselor: How many nights do you think it would be realistic for you to be on time?

Jim (After a pause.): Three?

Counselor: Susan, what would it be like if Jim was on time for dinner three nights a week?

Susan: That would be great. But I don't think he will do it.

Counselor: Maybe he will, and maybe he won't. We'll find out next session. But who knows? He may just decide to surprise you. It will be interesting to see what Jim chooses to do.

Jim (With a smile on his face and with a competitive tone in his voice.): Not only will I be on time, but if I'm going to be late, I will call you and let you know. How's that?

Susan (With a smile on her face.): Fat chance! But it would be nice!

Counselor: I'd like you to imagine a scale between one and ten. A one means that you are discouraged, dissatisfied and hopeless about your marriage. A ten means that most of the time you are pleased with your marriage, and that you enjoy high levels of satisfaction, good conflict resolution and deep levels of love and affection. How would you rate your marriage?

Susan (Responding immediately.): I'd give it about a three. I know that compared to some other couples our marriage isn't horrible. I mean, Jim doesn't beat me or anything. But when I compare it to what it could be, to what I think God would want it to be, I'm discouraged. Jim doesn't talk. He is negative and critical, and he always wants to go to Canada with his friend Don and fish for Northern Pike. I think that if things don't change, it's not worth going on.

Jim (With a surprised voice.): I didn't have any idea you thought it was that bad! I was going to say a seven.

Susan: A seven? Where have you been?

Counselor: Do you think you can do one more scale? Once again, I'd like you to imagine a scale between one and ten. This time a one means that you have virtually no commitment to making your marriage work. Quite frankly, if it falls apart today, that will be fine with you. A ten means that you would be will-

ing to invest whatever it takes, to do almost anything
to make your marriage the best it can be. How would
you rate your level of commitment?

Jim (Responding immediately.): I'm at a ten. I know I've
been slow in realizing how bad things are, but I am
committed to making our marriage all that God
designed marriage to be.

Susan (Looking at Jim, with a sarcastic tone in her voice.):
That's a pleasant surprise. *(Susan continues after a long
sigh.)* Well, in spite of how discouraged and frustrated I am, I would say that I'm probably at about a six.
I do love Jim, and I want our marriage to work, but
something has got to change.[6]

What I would like you to take from this quote are the two
requests the counselor asks the couple to work on before their
counseling begins. The first is for the couple to think about how
counseling could make a positive impact on their marriage. And
the second is for the couple to notice positive occurrences,
whether little or big, in the marriage. These are two key points I
will further discuss in the new approach.

A Traditional Method

Traditionally, many counselors and ministers have used the first
session, and even the second, to gather information and history
on the relationship. Personally, I see some difficulties with this
approach. While one spouse might be ready to discuss problems,
the other might not immediately want to tackle the main problems. And when just four or six sessions are scheduled and you
attempt to fit in an evaluation at this time, it eliminates the
already little time you have available for positive solutions and
growth.

Additionally, if the first session is devoted entirely to identifying the problems of the marriage, a pastor could be reinforcing a defeatist attitude about the marriage, which hinders progress. Most couples are well aware of their pain and conflict, and they have probably hashed it over for weeks and months before coming to see you. If anything is to be emphasized at this time, it should be strengths over weaknesses.

A New Approach

Instead of gathering assessment information and history on the relationship in one or two sessions, I suggest evaluating couples in a precounseling interview. The main purpose of this interview will be to build positive expectancies, establish a commitment for change and begin the process of change.

Since knowing the history and assessing the marriage are important, I suggest, not cutting this out of counseling, but

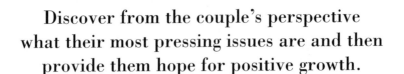

Discover from the couple's perspective what their most pressing issues are and then provide them hope for positive growth.

making it an interview and outside "homework" assignment by which you can evaluate a couple's marriage. Obtaining history and other key assessment information from both parties will help you avoid premature conclusions and suggestions that are not appropriate. Keep in mind that what you hear or read from one spouse will be biased, because each one tends to see himself or herself as more of an innocent victim than a villain.

History taking will help you discover any long-standing, consistent problems that might contribute to major issues revealed. Evaluating also helps you and the couple identify the strengths and positives that usually exist but are often over-looked. It is important to discover from the couple's perspective what the most pressing issues are. Then help the couple put the problems in context of the existing strengths and positive elements of the relationship.

The assessment information can be gathered outside of the marital interview by using *The Marriage Checkup Questionnaire,* which is a comprehensive inventory I created in order to help couples assess their marriage relationships.[7] Since some couples cannot verbally define their difficulties in specific objective terms and some are embarrassed to initially discuss certain topics with a pastor, responding to the questionnaire might prove easier for the couple. At the same time, the questionnaire will provide you a more complete picture of the relationship. Additionally, it is important to remind the couple that each spouse needs their own copy of the questionnaire in order that the couple individually reflects and responds to the inventory.

Your objective is to relieve pain and to provide hope for the possibility of positive growth. Picture yourself as a couple going for help. What would encourage you to return week after week? What would keep you going during the difficult times? What would encourage you to cooperate with the pastor?

By having the information beforehand, you can structure the first session according to the needs of the particular couple. You can assess their strengths, weaknesses, conflicts and areas of concern. You can also save several hours of counseling time by making the questionnaire a part of your approach.

THE QUESTIONNAIRE

The Marriage Checkup Questionnaire is a detailed inventory that helps a person express information concerning family structure and background, marriage preparation, personal information and marital evaluation—including tasks, qualities the person appreciates about his or her spouse, and requests and expectations each has for the other. What makes it unique from other inventories is that it ranks and evaluates specific areas of marriage like satisfaction and communication levels. Other topics include the couple's spiritual relationship, finances, decision-making and family issues.

The questionnaire will be very helpful to you because it will assist you in selecting a direction for a couple's session(s). It will reveal a person's goals for counseling, level of hopefulness for counseling, how much time a week can be devoted to marriage improvement, the amount of change the person is willing to make for marriage improvement, the person's level of commitment to stay in the marriage, as well as a spouse's perception of the other spouse's commitment level. The last two commitment items mentioned can very well dictate the directional emphasis in the initial session (see "Changes and Commitment Level" questions 4 and 5). For example, if one person is leaning toward commitment and one person is not, the counselor may need to devote more time and energy up front in attempts to get the spouse with a lower level of commitment to realize he or she needs to commit wholeheartedly in order for any progress to be made. This is necessary in order to encourage the less-committed spouse to stay in counseling, as well as to provide a sense of hope for the more-committed spouse that his or her spouse will change.

Having the couple complete this inventory serves several important purposes. Again, it provides for you most of the data needed for planning intervention prior to the first or second counseling session. It also helps the couple anticipate the subject matter that will occur in the session(s) based on what you find the couple needs to work on. Additionally, answers to the inventory questions initiate changes in the way spouses think about their objectives, sometimes resulting in change even before the first session. Because the questionnaire asks positive questions about strengths and what each one appreciates about the other, it helps each person see the marriage from a more balanced perspective. I have even had some couples decide not to come for counseling after completing the questionnaire because in the process they discovered their marriage was actually quite healthy and positive. The questionnaire revealed to the couple that they were overly concentrating on the problems, giving them the insight to stop and instead begin concentrating on the positives.

To best evaluate a couple, place each person's form side by side where you can quickly see areas of conflict, difference, concern, strength and weakness, all of which will help you formulate a specific counseling plan for a couple.

Following are some sample sections from *The Marriage Checkup Questionnaire*. In the first section, note the switching back and forth from the self-evaluation questions to the evaluation questions of the spouse. The specific questions help a person evaluate his or her relationship in particular aspects of the marriage. The questions also focus each person's thinking upon what he or she can do to change his or her own behavior for positive improvement. Finally, the questionnaire not only provides you insight into some of the critical areas of a marriage, but it also measures each spouse's level of importance to the other, and each spouse's own motivation and sense of responsibility.

Marital Evaluation

1. Describe how much significant time you spend together as a couple and when you spend it.
2. Describe five behaviors or tasks your spouse does that you appreciate.
3. List five personal qualities of your spouse that you appreciate.
4. How frequently do you affirm or reinforce your spouse for the behaviors and qualities described in questions 2 and 3?
5. List four important requests you have for your spouse at this time.
6. How frequently do you make these requests?
7. What is your spouse's response?
8. List four important requests your spouse has for you at this time.
9. How frequently does your spouse make these requests?
10. What is your response?
11. What do you appreciate about your spouse's communication?
12. What frustrates you the most about your spouse's communication?

Your Goals for Counseling

1. Describe your specific goals for counseling.
2. Describe your spouse's specific goals for counseling.
3. How long do you feel counseling should last (on a week-to-week basis)?

4. On the following scale, please indicate your level of hopefulness for the effectiveness of counseling. Use an *X* for yourself and a check mark for your perception of your spouse's hopefulness.

No hope					Hopeful				Very hopeful	
0	1	2	3	4	5	6	7	8	9	10

5. In what way can your minister/counselor be the greatest help to you in counseling? Please be specific.
6. How much time per week can you give to improve your marriage? Circle your response.

   1 hr.   2 hrs.   3 hrs.   4 hrs.   5 hrs.   6 hrs. or more

7. Would you like your minister/counselor to pray with you?
   ❑ Yes   ❑ No

   If yes,
   ❑ During the session?   ❑ During the week?

Changes and Commitment Level
Circle the word that best completes each statement.

1. I am willing to make **any, most, some, minor, very few** changes or adjustments necessary to improve our marriage together.
2. I believe my spouse is willing to make **any, most, some, minor, very few** changes or adjustments necessary to improve our marriage together.

3. It is **very important, somewhat important, not very important** to me that my spouse is satisfied and fulfilled.

4. My commitment level to improving my marriage is

Little or none					Average					Absolute
0	1	2	3	4	5	6	7	8	9	10

5. My spouse's commitment level to improving our marriage is

Little or none					Average					Absolute
0	1	2	3	4	5	6	7	8	9	10

It would be helpful for you to read through *The Marriage Checkup Questionnaire* as soon as possible to familiarize yourself with every part of it. Additional, detailed instructions are provided within the resource.

Chapter 2

BEFORE YOU DECIDE TO COUNSEL

As you have read so far, it is vital that one of your main goals before agreeing to counsel a couple is to measure and understand a couple's level of commitment. Most therapists begin to determine this by the end of the first or second session, but by using *The Marriage Checkup Questionnaire*, you have the information prior to the couple's first session with you. To keep counseling to six sessions or less, this idea of precounseling is a necessity. Again, the strategy you take or the plan you create for a couple's counseling will depend upon the couple's level of commitment, which is determined through the questionnaire.

It is highly likely that one day you will run across a couple or just one spouse in a precounseling session with a low level of commitment, or you will face another issue that requires you to decide if you should or should not counsel the couple or refer them to another staff member or professional therapist. Go to the Lord for guidance in these decisions, and He will help you decide if you need to decline or accept service for a couple.

WHEN TO MAKE A REFERRAL

Time Limitations

How much time do you have available for counseling? Are your counseling services available to the entire community or just to church members or attendees? Usually when a pastor or counselor answers "not much" to the first question and "to anyone" for the second question, this is when I highly recommend counseling couples in six sessions or less. Additionally, when the person or couple knows you have a set number of sessions, the progress can be more rapid. Keep in mind that every situation is unique, and you must make the decision of how you structure a couple's counseling, including how many sessions they need in order to improve. For example, a crisis situation will most likely take a longer period of time; therefore, you might need to assign more than six sessions.

When creating an outline for a couple's counseling sessions, remember that a more structured approach usually better helps the professional who is in a time bind. This is how it works: The professional asks each counselee, "How long do you want counseling to last—one month, three months, six months, a year?" Then they agree upon the time frame and finish the counseling in the allotted time. This way counselees usually work harder when they know just "so much" time is available. In other words, when counselees know they will have X number of sessions, rather than no set number, they make better use of their counseling time.

Complex Problems

If you sense that you have an extremely complex problem, you may want to give the couple a heads-up prior to the start of counseling. Inform them that at the end of your allotted number of sessions you will be referring them to a professional, but you are willing to work with them and help as much as possible in the meantime. That way if they prefer to have the referral right away, you can do so immediately, saving everyone time and energy.

Complex problems can also be beyond your expertise. We all have limitations; and we will be much better pastoral counselors by identifying, admitting and accepting our limitations. Limitations are not weaknesses. It is a sign of maturity to admit we cannot handle a certain problem and would like to pass it on to someone who can. While we would like to be all things to all people, this is not reality. Plainly and simply put: many ministers simply have not had sufficient training in their Bible college or seminary to handle many of the counseling issues brought forth to them.

Personality Differences and Emotional Attachments

Sometimes the match between you and the person or couple just doesn't work. It could be a conflict of personality or values, and you need to listen to the Holy Spirit if you feel Him cautioning you about counseling a particular relationship. On the other hand, the person or couple seeking your help could be personal friends or people you feel emotionally attached to. The best step in this situation is to find a competent professional for them and commit to pray for them regularly. You might also need to deal with your own personal feelings toward the situation by seeking counseling yourself. To find out how to cope with feeling like you are overly involved or already in over your head, I recommend reading *The Snare* by Lois Madow.[1]

WHAT APPROACH TO USE

Once you accept a couple's counseling request, you will need to make one more decision before your sessions begin—whether to work with the couple together or individually—and then choose an approach.

Working with a Couple Together

The following basic indicators can help you decide if you should see a couple together:

- If you have been working with both husband and wife individually and you do not see any carryover or effect upon the marriage
- If the relationship is explosive, and changes and agreements need to be made quickly
- If the couple has a need to enhance communication through nurturing and caring behaviors, the decision-making process or the sexual relationship
- If one person is suspicious or somewhat paranoid (meeting together will lessen the possibility of distortion or misrepresentation of what one or the other said, or of taking sides)

Basically, if a couple has the potential to accept, adapt and see each other's differences in a positive manner, working with the couple together will be more effective. It is ideal to see a couple together. And even if individual counseling is necessary, it can often be handled in the presence of the spouse. In fact, you will often find yourself alternating between a focus on the relationship and a focus on personal issues as you work with most couples.

Working with a Couple Separately

The following basic indicators can help you decide if you should see a couple separately:

- When one spouse needs to discuss any deviant behavior that is yet unknown to the spouse, seeing them alone is necessary. Confession, acknowledgment and deciding which direction to turn may take considerable time.
- If one spouse is totally weakened and shattered by the other spouse, or if his or her anxiety and tension level is so high that little productivity can occur, seeing the couple individually may help. It gives the dominated spouse a respite from the controlling, overpowering spouse.
- If severe mental disturbance is evident, a person is best seen individually. This kind of case is generally not handled by a pastor but is referred to a professional counselor. Making the referral may be done by having just the person present, or it might be best accomplished by having the spouse present for support.

Every couple and their situation is unique, so seek God's direction and then make your decision.

Choosing an Approach

Once you have a better sense of whether a couple needs counseling together or separately, you will need to choose an approach for your counseling sessions. Four of the more common approaches to working with couples both together and separately are as follows:

1. *Concurrent marital counseling or therapy.* Each person is seen individually by a counselor. From time to time, the sessions will include the couple together. Major problems involving marital issues are worked through at the same time.

2. *Conjoined marital counseling.* The couple is seen together by one or two counselors. This kind of counseling has a higher rate of success when both spouses desire help and are motivated to work. Often within the context of this counseling, individual work will occur in the presence of the other spouse.

3. *Individual counseling or therapy.* Each person is involved in counseling with either separate counselors or the same therapist. They do not meet together as a couple with the therapist. Sometimes during this approach the couple's relationship is dealt with, but it is not the major concern.

4. *Couples' group counseling or therapy.* This approach involves several couples meeting together with one or more counselors. This is often used to diffuse tension-filled relationships. Couples can learn from other couples' comments and by observing how they interact.

Remember, whether you decide to counsel a couple together or separately, your approach should be implemented prior to the first session in a precounseling interview and by having the couple fill out *The Marriage Checkup Questionnaire.*

GET TO KNOW YOUR COUNSELEES

Regardless of the plan you implement for any given couple, the significance of how you conduct the marital counseling cannot be overstated. A pastor needs to be an objective catalyst who is there to provide insight, guidance, hope and encouragement. He or she also needs to discover and nurture the abilities of the husband and wife. This is a big undertaking, isn't it? While we won't always succeed for a number of reasons, our role is still paramount.

What is our role? We must constantly study and learn, remain aware of who we do and don't work well with, be conscious of our own unresolved personal and marital issues, stay aware of why and what we say and do in counseling and finally, act as a reservoir of information, provide new insights and recommend resources to all couples.

THE FOUR PAIRS OF PREFERENCES

Over the past 30 years, I've become convinced that as counselors and ministers alike we need to model for the counselees what we are teaching or suggesting. We need flexibility in our approaches so that we can adapt to their thinking and communication styles. This is the crux of establishing rapport and moving ahead quickly. To accomplish this, we need to understand our own culture, generational bias, personality preferences, gender inclinations, and thinking and communication styles. Then based upon the knowledge of who we are and who the counselees are, we must adapt to speak their languages.

How can a 60-year-old therapist understand and relate to a young couple or a woman therapist understand and relate to a man's perspective? It takes study and work, but it is possible if you skill yourself in connecting to a person or couple through the language he or she speaks.

The book *Type Talk* by Otto Kroeger and Janet Thuesen has radically affected both my understanding of people and my counseling approach. The book is the clearest and most practical presentation of the Myers-Briggs Type Indicator that I have read. According to the theory behind this tool, each person has a preference early in life and sticks with it. The more these preferences are practiced, the more they are relied upon. You could say that these preferences are languages, and each person has their own way of communicating to others through these preferences.[1]

Extrovert Versus Introvert
Extrovert (E) or introvert (I) is the way a person prefers to interact with the world in order to receive stimulation and energy. In our society, extroverts outnumber introverts three to one.

An extrovert is energized by people and drained by solitude, but an introvert is drained by people and energized by solitude. Neither is wrong or right, but what happens in marriage to their social togetherness? An extrovert speaks first without any editing, whereas, the introvert needs to think it through first and then share a response. What happens in counseling if the counselor is an introvert and both husband and wife are extroverts? How do you help an extrovert and an introvert relate to one another? This is a common source of conflict for many couples.

Sensor Versus Intuitive

The second pair of preferences reflects the way people prefer to gather information. This particular preference will be explained further.

Thinker Versus Feeler

The third pair reflects how people prefer to make decisions, either as thinkers (T) or feelers (F). Two-thirds of American males prefer thinking decisions and two-thirds of American women prefer feeling decisions.

Judger Versus Perceiver

The fourth pair reflects how people prefer to orient their lives, either as structured and organized judgers or as spontaneous and adaptive perceivers.

A Sensor Versus an Intuitive

Most couples don't understand these differences when they marry, but time and time again I've seen couples develop acceptance and harmony in their marriages by reading *Type Talk*, even after being together for many years. The following descriptions of differences between one of the pairs of preferences—a sensor and an intuitive—are based on examples given in *Type Talk*.[2] Which one are you?

A Sensor

You are keyed in to information you receive through your five senses. What you pay attention to are the facts and details of situations. This is what you perceive or notice. It's what you believe.

What is it like to be a sensor? It really shows up in communication. When you ask a question, you want a specific answer (and that's the way you give answers). If you ask your spouse "What time should I meet you?" and she says "Around 4:00," that just won't do. You may reply, "Does that mean 3:55, 4:00 or 4:05?" You are that literal. I used to go fishing with a friend who was extreme in this regard. Anyone knows that when you ask your fishing partner if he or she has the bait, you're asking him or her to pass it to you. But when I'd ask Phil if he had the bait, he'd say "Yes," and that was it. He wouldn't pass the bait until I said, "Will you please pass the bait?" What you are doing is forcing others to be specific.

Another example is if a sensor were looking at something and thinking of purchasing it, and his or her spouse said, "It's a good deal; it's less than $100," the sensor would disregard this response. A sensor wants the bottom line. An adequate response from the spouse would've been, "It's a good deal; it's $91." Remember, the stronger your preference is in a particular pair, the more you are like this.

A sensor is a focused person. You have a high level of concentration on what you're presently doing. You deal with the future as it arrives and don't waste time wondering what's next.

You are a doer. If you have a choice between sitting around thinking about something or performing that task, there's no question as to what you'll do. You want to invest your efforts in tasks that yield visual results.

You're a factual person. Theories don't thrill you, but facts do. This probably affects the type and style of preaching or teaching you respond to. When you hear something from another person, you want it presented sequentially—A to B to C to D. You don't like it when others meander off the path.

Sensors have little use for fantasy. They wonder why people assume, speculate and imagine. What good does it do?

One of the biggest frustrations for sensors is when others don't give them clear guidelines or instructions. After all, they are very explicit and detailed. So it really bothers them when they receive instructions that are too general. If you ask a sensor, "Where's the nearest Starbucks coffee store?" he or she will say, "Turn around and go back out the way you came in. Turn left and go a block and a half to Seventeenth Street and turn left. It's three blocks down on the left, sandwiched between Kentucky Fried Chicken and a dry cleaners in a brick building." On the other hand, an intuitive would say, "Go to Seventeenth Street and turn left. It's a couple of blocks down on the right. You can't miss it."

Sensors also have difficulty seeing the big picture because they focus on their immediate task at hand. They see the individual tree but not the forest.

When it comes to money (which can be a source of major conflict in a relationship), sensors are very exacting. Money to them is tangible. When they have it, they use it, but only as much as the amount allows. They view money as a tool to be used. Sensors look at money realistically rather than through rose-colored glasses.

Finally, predictability in a relationship gives them a sense of security, whereas change throws them.

An Intuitive

The way you respond to the world is not through the five senses or by means of facts, but on the basis of your sixth sense or on hunches. Details and facts have their place (perhaps), but you can easily become bored with them. You don't take things at face value. Instead, you look for the underlying meaning of relationships. You look for possibilities. "Possibility" is a very important word to an intuitive whose focus is not on the here and now but on the future.

Intuitives are sometimes perceived as a bit absentminded. Why? Simply because they like to think of several things at once. Sometimes it's difficult to concentrate on what's going on at the moment because the future has so many intriguing possibilities. Intuitives live for the future. Today's purpose is to get ready for tomorrow! If an intuitive is going on a trip somewhere, he or she already started experiencing the vacation weeks before, while the sensor doesn't experience it until arriving at the destination.

There is another significant difference between a sensor and an intuitive. When the intuitive describes something, it's as though he or she is experiencing the description.

One couple I know had these different preferences. Jim was an intuitive, and Sheila was a sensor. Jim had traveled a great deal in college, but Sheila had never left Nebraska until she married.

They were married a little over a year when Jim told her of the dream vacation he wanted them to take the next summer. He wanted to explore Canada and Alaska. He told her of the possibility (there's that word again) of getting another couple to go with them. He described what it would be like to drive from San Diego all the way to Vancouver, B.C., and then work their way to Anchorage, Alaska. It wouldn't cost that much since they could take tents and sleeping bags and stay in campgrounds all the way. He told her of the places and signs of wildlife they would see and experience. The more he talked, the more expressive and involved he became (it was almost real to him in his description).

By the time Jim finished, he was expecting Sheila to be just as enthusiastic as he was. It didn't happen. She was anything but thrilled with the idea, since her practical preference saw all sorts of problems. The questions rolled out one after the other: "How can we afford to take the time?" "What if the car breaks down?" "Is it really safe to camp?" "Where will we eat?" "What about showers?"

Jim felt crushed. He had thought Sheila would respond the way he felt. He had shared a dream with her. He hadn't said, though, it was a dream; rather, he had presented it as though it would happen. Sheila had taken everything he said literally and felt overwhelmed. If Jim had presented the trip in her language—in a factual manner—and had anticipated her questions and given detailed answers, she would have responded more favorably. Jim had been communicating as if he were talking with another intuitive.

Intuitives have a unique way of dealing with time—to them it's relative. They may have a watch, but it doesn't help them to be on time. "Late" doesn't register unless an event has started without them. They may also be late because they tried to do too much; they thought they could complete those five tasks before they had to leave for the meeting.

Can you begin to see how a sensor and an intuitive might be attracted to one another? The staunch, staid, responsible one may admire the free-spirited butterfly. But can you also see the potential for driving each other up the wall after the infatuation and honeymoon bliss wear off?

Which of these preferences do you relate to the most? How well do you understand and connect with a person of the opposite preference? What recommendations can you give to a sensing wife and an intuitive husband or vice versa, so they can learn to relate to one another? How can you help them activate the less-dominant preference in relating to one another? How do you help them change once they understand?

These questions need to be answered and can be as you learn to use these principles. My book *Communication: Key to Your Marriage* will give you an overview as well as information concerning preferences and how those affect our communication styles.[3] You will soon find yourself asking couples to read this book.

THE THREE SENSES

As people grow and mature they develop their own ways of perceiving life. They take in or respond to life through a particular response system. The system processes information and makes sense out of life. Sense is referred to as a person's style of communication or language, and the different systems are visual, audio and kinesthetic. The following communication approach I highlight is based on Robert Dilts's *Applications of Neuro-Linguistic Programming* (NLP).[4] However, we will skim the surface in order to provide you a glimpse of the senses.

People who are more visually oriented primarily use remembering and thinking to process life around them. An auditorily oriented person is one who listens to life and depends upon spoken words for his or her information source. A kinesthetically oriented person feels his or her way through life experiences. His or her feelings determine the response.

For many years my dominant mode—how I see life and respond to it—has been visual. If a secretary comes in and says, "Here's an interesting letter, let me read it to you," without thinking I usually say, "Oh, let me see it." I process it faster and comprehend it better if I read it myself. However, over the years I have developed the auditory and feeling systems more because I have practiced responding to all of my senses. In many situations we cannot respond by using a visual mode; therefore, we must use either the auditory or kinesthetic mode.

This is my story of how I was able to break free from just using my natural visual sense. I was raised as a typical male in our American culture. I had no male model of emotional expression, so for many years I was emotionally stunted. My son, Matthew, who is retarded, was the instrument God used to break open that part of my life and motivate me to feel. Through the many experiences I had with him for almost 23 years, I felt the entire gamut of emotions in depth, including intense emotional frustration and pain. I cherish those experiences because I now respond more fully to life, to others and to God because of them. Now, I can also feel and speak the language of the one who naturally speaks kinesthetically.

Differentiate the Senses

How do you determine a person's dominant response system? It is simple. Listen to the words he or she uses—the adjectives, verbs, predicates and descriptives. People will tell you all you need to know through their words.

Here are some visual phrases: "I *see* what you're saying." "That *looks* like a good idea." "*Show* me more about it." "It's kind of *hazy* at this time." "Let's get a new *perspective*." "Let's shed some *light* on this." "Let's *focus* in on this." "What's your *point of view?*"

Here are some auditory examples: "That's as clear as a *bell*." "This *sounds* good to me." "Can't you *tune in* to what I'm saying?" "*Tell* me that again." "That's coming through *loud and clear*." "I *hear* you."

Here are some kinesthetic examples: "I have a good *feeling* about this." "I *sense* you're upset with me." "This day has a good *feel* to it." "Can you *grasp* what this means?" "That's a *heavy* problem." "Can you get *in touch* with that?"

Listen to what is said (that's auditory) and you will begin to see (that's visual) what they are sensing (that's kinesthetic) about their situation. Here are some illustrations to show what happens when we do not use the other person's sense:

First Person: If you would *look* over what I've written, you would *see* that I have really *focused* on the main issues. I don't *see* what the problem is. (Visual)

Second Person: I get the *feeling* that something is missing. I am trying to *sense* what it is, but I'm still missing it. (Kinesthetic)

First Person: Well, I think you're just locked into your *point of view*. *Look* at it from my *perspective*, will you? (Visual)

Second Person: I don't think you're in *touch* with the main problem. (Kinesthetic)

What are these two people doing? They are using their individual senses to communicate with one another, and since the senses are different, they are not understanding one another.

Let's look at another miscommunication.

First Person: I want to *talk* to you. I've got some ideas *rattling* about and I would like to know how they *sound* to you. (Auditory)

Second Person: Let's *look* at what you've got. Have you *written* them down for me? (Visual)

First Person: No. I'm just starting to *tune* in to them myself. I guess I want to use you as a *sounding board* first. It's still not too clear even to me. (Auditory)

Second Person: Well, I'm pretty busy. When you have something to *show* me, then I can *focus* in and *see* what *direction* to go. (Visual)

Again, miscommunication occurs because neither person "sees" or "hears" the other's communication.

Now here is an example of clear communication. Notice the responses of the "Pacer."

First Person: As I *look* over this paper you've *written*, I find some *unclear* areas in it. I am a bit *fuzzy* about what you are trying to communicate. (Visual)

Pacer: Yes. I think I *see* what you're getting at. Let me try to *paint a picture* of it for you and then we might *see* eye to eye on it. (Visual Response)

Second Person: I think we need to *talk* about this some more. I've *listened* to your concerns about the kids, but I'm not sure that we're on the same *wavelength*. (Auditory)

Pacer: Well, I think I can *tune* in to what you're *saying*. Let's go back and do a *replay* of what we're *saying* and it will become clearer. (Auditory)

Third Person: "I'm not in *touch* with what you're trying to communicate. I don't *feel* comfortable with this and I wonder about it. I don't *sense* the direction." (Kinesthetic)

These concepts may be new to you, but they are the basis for relating to others effectively. Have you listened to your sermons or lessons? What kinds of words do you use? What is your dominant mode? Remember that the congregation or class you minister to is made up of all three perceptual modes. You may want to rewrite some of your messages and experiment so that you speak the congregation's languages, which include all three senses. You might be surprised at the results.

Here is an illustration of how this approach is used in business. Below are three different realty descriptions of the same house. The real estate agent has described it in different ways, depending upon the prospective buyer's perceptual mode. As you read these descriptions, which one appeals to you? It may tell you something about your dominant mode.

A: This house is *picturesque*. It has a quaint *look* about it. You can *see* that a lot of *focus* has been put on the *colorful* patio and garden area. It has a lot of window space so you can enjoy the *view*. It is *clearly* a good buy. (Visual)

B: This house is *soundly* constructed and situated. It is such a *quiet* area that all you'll *hear* when you walk outside are the *sounds* of the birds *singing*. Its storybook interior has so much character you'll probably *ask* yourself how you could ever pass it by. (Auditory)

C: This house is not only solidly constructed, it has a special *feel* to it as well. It's not often you come in contact with a place that *touches* on so many features. It is spacious enough so that you really *feel* you can move around *freely*, yet *cozy* enough so that you won't *wear yourself out* taking care of it. (Kinesthetic)

Do you notice the differences? Focus on the italicized words, and you will soon discover the differences.

Here are some words to help you identify what response system is being communicated.

> *Visual:* focus, see, clear, bright, picture, perspective, show, hazy, colorful, pretty, peak, glimpse
> *Auditory:* listen, yell, talk, hear, harmony, noisy, discuss, call, loud, shout, told
> *Kinesthetic (Feeling):* feel, firm, touch, pressure, sense, concrete, hurt, touchy, irritated, clumsy, relaxed

As you familiarize yourself with these words, you will find yourself better identifying the sense in which your counselees communicate. It will also help you in your own personal relationships. For example, we don't use adult language and phrases with a small child who does not have the same experiences, vocabulary and manner of reasoning we have. In a similar fashion, we can't expect other people to really understand us unless we move into their world. Too many ministers and counselors expect the counselees to adapt to *them.*

Too often I've heard messages that reflect the minister's own personality and thinking orientation, and then he or she wonders why only a certain segment of the congregation was reached by the message. I've also heard other ministers who reach a large segment because they blend visual, auditory and kinesthetic words to amplify a point or present it condensed, give illustrations and provide descriptions using both feeling and cognitive terminology. This conveys to a congregation that the minister understands the value orientation of the 60-year-olds as well as those in their 30s. Consider this final principle as a summary: In relationships, the person with the widest range of responses will have the greatest influence and control.

Effective Communication Styles

Discover Your Counselee's Style of Communication

We need to discover as counselors our counselee's sense and then communicate it back to him or her in the same way. The principle is this: If I speak his or her language, real listening and change can occur. The couple or individual will learn to communicate effectively back to you when you model his or her style of expression.

Where do you do this? Focus in on the counselee's style of communication at the precounseling interview before you even begin the counseling sessions. This is important, since you want to be as effective as possible from the very onset of your time together.

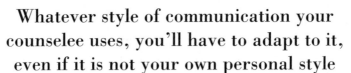

Whatever style of communication your counselee uses, you'll have to adapt to it, even if it is not your own personal style of communication.

How do you do this? Try to discover whether the counselee is visually, auditorily or kinesthetically (feeling) oriented by listening to the tone and volume of the voice and the phrases he or she uses. In other words, study his or her nonverbal communication. For example, some people are loud, expressive and gesture a lot. Others are quiet, reserved, proper and choose their words carefully. Some are expanders while others are condensers. Some are ramblers while others are concise and to the point. Whatever style of communication your counselee uses, you'll have to adapt to it, even if it is not your own personal style of communication. You'll be amazed at how much rapport, trust and cooperation will build between counselor and counselee as a result of your adaptation.

Discover Your Style of Communication

Yes, you just heard the word "adapt." This means you will need to become aware of your own style of communication. First, you will need to educate yourself on the different styles of communication in order to make the shift. For example, expanding your vocabulary and changing tone and volume are all possible changes you'll need to make. Second, you will need to be flexible in order to quickly change from one style to another. Look at the following example illustrating one of my adaptation experiences.

Several years ago, before I had read any material about this communication approach, I discovered its effectiveness with a couple of my clients. I was seeing a young couple from a traditional Italian family, or tribe, as they called themselves. They were outgoing, loud and exuberant. They interrupted one another, outshouted one another, were full of enthusiasm and used a lot of gestures. In the first two sessions I got nowhere with them. Instead of listening to me, they interrupted and ignored me. I was getting more and more frustrated. Before the third session with them I thought, *The way I'm conducting my counseling isn't working. I need to do something different.* They weren't responding to my style of communication, so I decided to communicate as they did.

When the third session started, I raised my voice along with theirs, interrupted them and used their tone of voice and gestures. It worked wonderfully! They responded to me and we understood one another. I would lean forward, interrupt Tony and say, "Tony! Tony! Listen to Mary. She's got something to say. Mary, tell him again." And my hands were gesturing for Tony to relax and listen to Mary. As they left, Tony turned and shook my hand and said, "Great session today, Norm, great session." From that session on we really worked well together. I found that I really looked forward to the sessions with them. And I enjoyed discovering that the counselor needs to adapt to the communication style of his or her counselees.

Do you see how I began establishing rapport in the third session of counseling? I did so by adapting to the couple's communication style. However, again, I recommend that you start the rapport right from the first session. During the first session, be perceptive and take notice if your communication is being accepted or rejected by the counselee. You can do this by reading the person's verbal and nonverbal language and his or her responses to you. If you are communicating effectively, you don't have to make any adjustments. If not, you need the flexibility to change and to do something different. If you would like the other person to change, you must change your own responses first. The counselee will usually change in response to the change he or she perceives in you. By becoming more flexible, you will have more influence upon others.

Implement the Change
Here are two important steps to follow in your counseling after you determine the counselee's style of communication: pacing and speaking the counselee's verbal language.

Pacing simply means meeting the other person where he or she is and matching his or her communication style. Pacing can mean picking up the mood, body language and speech patterns, which include tone of voice, volume, mood and language. In a sense, pacing means responding to another person as though you were a mirror reflection of that person.

For example, if you happen to be an "up" kind of person, friendly and chipper, and a counselee comes in "down" and distressed, your mood may make the person feel you are not sensing what he or she is experiencing. I don't mean for you to act depressed, but endeavor to match the volume, rate of speech and tone to show that you are catching what the person is feeling.

I'm an alert, ready-to-go person in the morning. Not everyone is. I remember one staff member with whom I worked for two years who was alert and energetic—but not at nine o'clock in the morning. It took me awhile to realize she could not handle an overload of information presented with a lot of intensity and rapidity first thing in the morning. I had to slow down and pace myself until she "came alive." Then at times it was all I could do to keep up with her! Sensitivity to your staff, as well as your counselees, will make your communication much more effective and, thus, will build rapport, trust and cooperation.

In essence, when you speak the other person's language, you are pacing. You are saying "I'm with you," "I can be trusted" and "I accept you."

Speaking the counselee's verbal language involves saying and expressing words that are similar to his or her language. For example, some people speak in short, brief sentences. Others give elaborate explanations. First listen to how the presentation is actually made, and then attempt to duplicate it. When I work with couples, I find that one spouse often gives two-line summaries and the other spouse gives a four-minute description. You might guess that when I speak to the summarizer I keep it brief; and when I speak to the elaborator, I use more detail.

Let's look at a summarizer husband and an elaborator wife, which is usually the case for many couples. I try to teach the couple that when the husband is speaking to his wife, he should use her language and give more detail. And I suggest to the wife that when speaking to her husband, she should use his language and keep it brief. This teaches them flexibility. Your task is to custom design your own communication in order to reach both spouses. In other words, you become a translator for both styles of communication, helping the couple connect and understand one another.

In marriage counseling, I have no doubt that you will encounter couples with different preferences and senses. The couples will speak different languages with words of different meanings. It is your goal as the counselor and translator to convey to the couples that when each spouse learns to speak the other spouse's language, then and only then will they be able to communicate and make significant progress with one another. This concept will make sense to the couple eventually, so keep the faith!

Chapter 4

PAVE THE WAY FOR CHANGE

Session One

Two popular counseling methods that I feel are key for marital counseling to succeed in six sessions or less are the behavior and thoughts approach and the solution-focused approach. And it is at the first session where these two approaches need immediate implementation. Why? Because an early introduction to the approaches paves the way for change in the following sessions.

THE BEHAVIOR AND THOUGHTS APPROACH

When couples come for counseling, is the emphasis placed on their behavior, thoughts or feelings? All three are significant and need to be acknowledged. However, I'm suggesting a model based on behavior and thoughts. Keep in mind that the model does not deny the existence or validity of a person's feelings; it simply does not focus directly on feelings as the source of marital conflict. Feelings will still be expressed throughout the entire counseling period.

One goal to work toward in this model is to first have the couple gain respect for one another's feelings. When this has been accomplished, the husband and wife have a better chance to focus on the problem behaviors without judging each other. Therefore, each spouse will more likely address behaviors they can and should change.

Behavior Versus Thoughts

I have found more often than not that immediate change in the marital relationship is more probable when the counselor first works on behavioral problems with couples. Usually, behavior is easier to change than thoughts, because behavior is voluntary and can be changed at will by the person, while thoughts are often involuntary, automatic or highly refined (even though they do initiate behavior).

Behavior changes are usually the catalysts for changing thoughts. A change in a person's behavior affects not only his or her own thoughts and feelings, but those of his or her spouse as well. Plus, changes of behavior can be recognized more easily. How do you know a spouse has changed his or her thoughts? Either through his or her behavior or verbal recognition.

Remember the following points in the counseling office when using the behavior and thoughts approach:

1. A person or couple is encouraged to change their behavior with an increase of positive behaviors regardless of their attitude and feelings.
2. A change in attitude or thought needs to occur early, based on the belief that a change in behavior will effect a change in feelings.

3. Behavior is easier to change because it is voluntary. Often thoughts are automatic, although many behaviors do stem from intentional thoughts.

4. It is important for a person to focus upon his or her thought life (or what sometimes is called "self-talk") while making a change in behavior.

5. Often it is difficult for a counselor to determine whether a person or couple should focus on changing thoughts first or behaviors first. Therefore, counselors need to discuss with the counselees both options in order to determine where to start.

6. Whenever possible, changes or solutions should occur on the part of both spouses. Those who are not alone in having to do all the work are more willing to change. When two are involved, each benefits from the other's feedback and assistance. Also, each person's participation can be a positive reinforcement for the positive changes the other person is attempting. Each person's behavior is directly related to the other person's behavior, and mutual change has a greater opportunity to become permanent. Think about this in your own life. Do you make changes more willingly when others respond positively? Probably.

As you begin the first session by talking with distressed couples regarding their behavior, you will soon discover that loving behaviors between them are most likely limited or noncreative, and they have been this way for many years. The couple's value on positive behaviors has most likely diminished and lost its significance. Therefore, new and creative responses must be discovered and deployed.

The Positive Way to Change

In his book *Why Marriages Succeed or Fail,* Dr. John Gottman suggests that a key ingredient in stable marriages is the negative and positive responses between husband and wife. If the ratio is five to one in favor of positive responses, he concludes that the marriage, despite the couple's possibly differing communication styles, tends to be stable.[1]

What are some positive responses? They include showing interest, a listening ear, affection, thoughtfulness, appreciation, concern, empathy, acceptance, laughter and joy.[2]

If research does indicate these are determining factors of marital stability, then assisting couples to learn to develop their positive responses may create solutions for problem behaviors. There is also biblical teaching showing that we need to overcome negativity and sin through positive behaviors. Consider these passages:

> I therefore, the prisoner for the Lord, appeal to and beg you to walk (lead a life) worthy of the [divine] calling to which you have been called [with behavior that is a credit to the summons to God's service, living as becomes you] with complete lowliness of mind (humility) and meekness (unselfishness, gentleness, mildness), with patience, bearing with one another *and* making allowances because you love one another (Eph. 4:1-2, *AMP*).

> Be kind and compassionate to one another, forgiving each other, just as in Christ God forgave you (Eph. 4:32).

> Therefore, as God's chosen people, holy and dearly loved, clothe yourselves with compassion, kindness, humility, gentleness and patience. Bear with each other and forgive whatever grievances you may have against

one another. Forgive as the Lord forgave you. And over all these virtues put on love, which binds them all together in perfect unity. Let the peace of Christ rule in your hearts, since as members of one body you were called to peace. And be thankful (Col. 3:12-15).

One of the main reasons to accelerate the rate in which spouses exchange positive behaviors in the first session is to help them move into a position of readiness for more changes that might prove more difficult in upcoming sessions.

The Positives Will Succeed

Before spouses are ready to negotiate major issues, they must first be convinced that the relationship is worth it. They need to know they will receive positive interaction from their spouse. So the first session is designed to provide spouses with an immediate "shot in the arm" of marital satisfaction, in order to fill up

Before spouses are ready to negotiate major issues, they must first be convinced that the relationship is worth it.

their empty storehouse of benefits as well as energy. If successful, this intervention makes spouses aware of the worth of their relationship. It encourages them to persevere through the remaining counseling sessions with you.

This is again why our first stress in counseling will be to

identify and emphasize positive behaviors that will build the marital relationship. This is why receiving *The Marriage Checkup Questionnaire* completed prior to the first session is so important—it will help you identify the problem behaviors and thoughts and bring them to the couple's attention.

The principle behind emphasizing the positive behaviors is that it drowns out the negative. For example, I have couples tell me in the waiting room that a 45-minute session won't be time enough to tell me all their marital difficulties. However, instead of letting the couple rant and rave about their problems, I ask each one to summarize in three minutes through writing or a drawing the positive benefits, special times and experiences they appreciate about one another in their marriage relationship. What is the result? Many couples end up realizing that their marriage was in better shape than they thought. They realize that by just focusing on the negatives, they were ignoring the positives. And this is the case with many couples today.

Your task is to help a couple discover their positive behaviors through three factors within their marriage relationship:

1. existing strengths and positive responses;
2. positive areas the couple would like to increase;
3. areas of agreement between the couple.

Be on the lookout when emphasizing the positive, because some couples will be both surprised and resistant when the negative areas are deemphasized. They might hesitate or not be up front with their responses. Others might breathe a sigh of relief. Comments and reactions at this time might include:

- "This isn't what I thought we would talk about."
- "How will this help? It's his drinking and running

around that's the problem."
- "I guess what you've suggested sounds a bit risky to me. What if I cooperate and do this and there is no response from him?"

Remember to convey to your counselees that risk is involved when you highlight the positives. For some couples, this focus upon the positive rather than the negative could be perceived as a threat. Why? Because most couples come to marital counseling

Direct the couple to identify positive qualities within their marriage, which will provide them a firm foundation to build their relationship.

expecting to talk about the problems, irritating behaviors or negative attitudes of the other person. The problem with this approach is that focusing on the negatives usually consumes all available energy, as the conflicts soon loom out of proportion.

Do not allow the couple to control the direction of counseling if you sense they want to dwell on the negatives. Progress is hindered when this happens. Instead, direct the couple to identify positive qualities within their marriage. This provides them with a firm foundation on which they can build their relationship, and at the same time it develops a more realistic perspective.

THE SOLUTION-FOCUSED APPROACH

Solution-focused counseling is a relatively new, simple, structured, positive approach that has proven effective in getting couples' marriages back on track. It is a departure from traditional approaches to counseling. In the first half of the last century, the emphasis in counseling was on the question, What is the cause of the problem? When the cause was discovered, then an intervention was planned. The problem was not that a variety of traditions and schools of thought looked for the cause of the problems, but that they all seemed to arrive at different answers. Then during the 1950s, counselors began to ask a different question: What maintains the problem—what keeps it going? Again, like the first question, an intervention could only be planned after the cause was discovered.

However, in more recent years a different question is being asked: How do we construct solutions? A pastor-counselor with this emphasis would approach a couple with the intention of first discovering what they wanted, or the intervention, rather than focusing on what they did not want, or the problems. The couple needs to determine what works and then concentrate on that area. If what they are doing doesn't work, then your job is to help them discover something that does work. This is similar, in some ways, to other approaches in this book but is more refined.

Take a look at the following example of one man who achieved success by focusing on what worked. One of the leading hitters for the Chicago Cubs a few years ago had fallen into a batting slump and was desperately trying to break out of it. The manager, Jim Frey, noticed what his player was trying to do to break the slump. The player was watching films of himself at bat. The only problem was that he was watching films of the times when he was in a slump. He was trying to find the cause of the problem. He thought if he could find out what he was doing wrong, then he could correct his mistake. But by watching the problematic videos, he only succeeded in learning in more detail how to continue batting poorly, therefore prolonging the slump. Finally the player decided to begin watching films showing him in a hitting streak. Guess what? He immediately began to improve.

This newer approach to counseling believes not only in focusing on what works but also that more than one solution exists and that the solutions can be constructed, rather than discovered. However, it takes the minister and the counselees working together to construct the possible solutions.[3]

What it comes down to is that this approach is a simple one. Its underlying premise is that it will provide you the best success rate within the time constraints you face. My recommendation is this: When counseling a couple in six sessions or less, approach each session as if you were only going to see the couple that one time. This will help you stay extremely focused and on track, and it will help you consider other important questions such as: How can I assist this couple spiritually if I am only going to see them once? If I could help them apply just one passage from God's Word to their marriage, what would it be? How can I assist them in developing a plan to improve their marriage if they are not returning to counseling? Again, I can't emphasize enough how vital it is to have the couple complete *The Marriage Checkup Questionnaire* prior to their first session. If you do, you will have an easier time implementing this solution-focused approach because of the vast amount of information you will already have.

Goal Setting

At the heart of the solution-focused approach to counseling are two important concepts—goal setting and hypothetical solutions and exceptions. We will first discuss how discovering the goals of your counselees will tell you how the couple desires to improve their relationship, thus establishing the opportunity for you to plan their remaining counseling sessions in a focused, detailed manner.

First, you'll need to discover the couple's goals through carefully worded questions. No one question is perfect, so you will have to adapt and experiment. A basic question that can be asked in many ways is, What is your goal in coming to see me? In other words, how does the couple want their marriage to be different? What do they want to have happen because of your time together? This is an important question because it conveys the message at the heart of this approach—goal development. This means that the topic of your discussions together is solution talk, rather than problem talk. Your goal as a counselor is to get your counselees to talk about what they want to accomplish, rather than who is at fault.

Think of it this way. Twice in my life I've been caught in a river's mud, a quicksand-like substance. It was a scary, frustrating experience. Your first inclination is to fight and struggle, but the more you struggle, the deeper you sink. Many marital problems are like quicksand. So the more you let a couple fight against a problem, the more entrenched they become in the throes of the problem. In other words, it grows, rather than goes away.

Since many couples have only a vague understanding of goal setting, it is your job to explain its benefits. To some the concept is foreign, so at times you might feel as if you're teaching someone a new language. For others, the concept might already be established in their daily lives. Some people move through life making things happen because they set goals. Others move through life drifting, having no clear direction, letting events and situations direct them. Some personality types love goal setting, where others see it as a dirty word. You may have to teach a person or couple what a goal is and how to construct it. They may call it by a different name such as a dream, desire and so on. Whatever the case may be, you want to explain to couples that their goals should express what they want to achieve through

Explain to couples that their goals should express what they want to achieve through counseling.

counseling.

Goals are descriptions of what we want to achieve in counseling—a clear picture of the anticipated result of therapy. Most people, when they seek help, hope the counselor will make them better. Sadly enough, some counselors and ministers actually avoid goal setting because it takes work to motivate counselees to set goals. However, if goals are not set, it may keep the counseling process from going anywhere purposeful. Keep in mind that a goal is a description or clear picture of what the couple wants to accomplish in counseling. Goals need to answer the questions of who is going to do what, when, where, with or to whom and to what extent.

Here is your very own step-by-step list of how you can make this practice a reality in your counseling office.

1. *Setting goals focuses the attention on action.* New perspectives give counselees a vision toward which they can direct their energies. Those who have goals are less

likely to engage in aimless behavior.

2. *Setting goals mobilizes energy and effort.* Clients who seem to drag their feet during a discussion of problems may come to life when faced with the question of spelling out alternatives. Goal setting is not just a mental exercise; people begin moving toward goals in a variety of ways once they are set.

3. *Setting goals increases persistence.* Not only are people who have goals motivated to do something, but they also tend to work harder and longer. Counselees who have clear and realistic goals don't give up as easily as those who have vague or no goals at all.

4. *Setting goals leads naturally to search for the means to accomplish them.* Once the goal is set and an assessment of the current condition made, the difference may seem far smaller than imagined. This can mobilize resources that were dormant to that point.[4]

Now with these four steps fresh in your mind, go ahead and read the following example of a wife's actual counseling session where the counselor has adopted this approach:

Therapist: What is your goal in coming here *(elicitation of a goal)*?

Wife: We have been having difficulties. A few years ago my husband quit his job to go back to school, and I took over the financial responsibilities. Lately I have been feeling overwhelmed with all the responsibilities. In addition to the responsibilities, I placed his needs ahead of mine because that's what I've always done, but last weekend I decided that I had had enough. I began feeling overwhelmed, so I left him and went to stay with my sister. *(Notice that despite the goal-oriented question from the counselor, sometimes clients will begin anyway with complaints or problems. Often, within these statements, there are hints of exceptions and differences.)*

Therapist: Was it different for you to take that kind of action *(exception elicitation and looking for contextual differences)*?

Wife: Yes, very much so, and things have been a little better since then. I have moved back in, but I told him that there were things I wanted him to do differently, like that we need to communicate differently, and he has listened and been more open with me. *(Client expands on the exception and how this action on her part is very different.)*

Therapist: Really *(with encouraging tones and curiosity)*? How have you seen him do that *(specification)*?

Wife: Well, in the past he would walk away, but now he really listens, and is actually encouraging me to say more. I also wanted him to find a job, and he has been looking. I also asked him to come to therapy, and the fact that he is here means a lot to me.

Therapist: I guess it does *(with encouraging tone)*; it is not always easy to come to therapy. Well, let me ask this: If you continued to have these good talks, and you continued to think more often of yourself first, would you think you were on track to getting what you want from coming here? *(Bridging the exception as the goal of therapy, and using her words as much as possible.)*

Wife: Yes.

The counselor's approach continues with the wife's husband,

who has agreed to seek help.

> Therapist (*With enthusiasm.*): Is this true; have you been doing all these things (*exception elicitation*)?
>
> Husband: Yes I have, but it has been hard. For a long time, the role reversal has been extreme. She has been taking care of the bills and sometimes not too well. When she would mess up the bills, I just did not want to know. I figured that if she messed them up, then she would have to clean them up. But lately I figured that we have to work together, so I got myself involved again (*expands on exception and offers the new meaning he is operating under, "We have to work together"*).
>
> Therapist: So you decided that not being involved was not working, and so you decided to try something new by getting more involved with the finances. That is really great. How are you doing that (*eliciting contextual differences and specification*)?
>
> Husband: Well, when she left for those few days, I realized how important she is to me and that I cannot just leave all the headaches to her anymore (*new meaning*).
>
> Therapist: How has she been different (*exception elicitation about her*)?
>
> Husband: I have pushed for more of what is changing and no more of what wasn't working, which for her was to keep things from me just to keep the peace. She has told me more about what she wants me to do and how bad things really are financially.
>
> Therapist: I guess her leaving was quite a shock to you?
>
> Husband: Yes, it was.

Therapist: Well, I am impressed that you went ahead and did something about it. Not everybody does, and you could have just let her go *(encouraging and reinforcing)*. So, are there other things you are doing that she has not noticed yet *(elicitation and specification with the expectation that there are other exceptions)*?

Husband: Yes, I contacted my sister about a loan for us. I had to eat my pride because I am a pretty private person.

Therapist: I can see that it was hard. I guess that indicates how serious this situation is to you and how much you care to get things back on track. If you continue to do these things and the two of you continue to have these open and good talks, even if talking is not always easy, would you think you are on track to getting what you want out of coming here *(bridging the exceptions as the goal of therapy)*?

Husband: Yes, I think so.

Therapist: Well then, let me ask, how are the two of you going to keep doing these things *(pursuing the exceptions as the goal of therapy)*?[5]

To start using this goal-setting approach, it is important to adapt the certain criteria in order to achieve well-defined goals for the couples and individuals you help.

First, goals need to be stated in terms of what the couple will be doing or thinking, rather than what they won't be doing or thinking. You don't want them to reinforce the problem but, rather, the solution. When they leave, you want them thinking about what can be accomplished, rather than what cannot be done. When a person talks about a negative or a problem, the way to shift his or her thinking is to ask "What would you like to be doing instead?" or "What do you see yourself doing instead that would be more beneficial?" This is what I would call pursuing, or bridging, the exceptions to a particular problem.

Second, the goals need to be stated in an ongoing way or process. When the couples begin using verbs ending in "ing," they have a greater likelihood of growth. This includes phrases such as the following:

- "I will be listening"
- "I will be or would be complimenting"

To accomplish this, instead of asking a couple *what* they will do differently (and you may need to at first), ask *how* they will respond differently. *How* promotes action and causes them to think in order to implement growth and change.

Third, goals need to focus on what can be done immediately, in the here and now, as opposed to in the future. You want couples to begin working and changing immediately, and this is what makes counseling couples in six sessions or less possible. One of the phrases used frequently is "on track," as in "If you are on track this week in your communication, what will you be doing differently?" Such a question should help elicit an answer that shows the person or couple implementing a change. Remember, the more immediate the goal, the greater the possibility of attainment.

Fourth, make the goals as specific as possible. It is important to assist the couple in making their goals as specific as possible to what they will be thinking and doing. Here again you can see the emphasis on both behavior and thoughts, as discussed previously in the chapter. This goal-setting step will probably take the most time to implement during the first session. And keep in mind that people's differing preferences and senses, their styles of communication, will affect how you counsel a couple into their specific goals. For example, if one spouse is introverted, it is important that you add the phrase "Think about this for a minute, will you?" to your question. This not only better aids the introverted spouse in creating their specific goals, but it also serves as a model for the extroverted spouse on how he or she should communicate to his or her introverted spouse.

Here is an example of being specific: A husband once told me he wanted his wife to be more loving toward him, and he wanted to meet her needs more. I asked him what he meant by this, and he was finally able to say:

- "I want my wife to touch me tenderly several times a day."
- "I want my wife to tell me she loves me each day."
- "I will ask my wife each day how I can meet her needs that day."
- "I will put my things away when I get home because I know she would appreciate that."

In order for your counselees to achieve this level of expression, you need to continually emphasize the importance of detail.

However, in some cases, the individual or couple is very capable of detailed responses but for one reason or another holds back and express themselves using vague terms. Usually these people are describing a problem and would rather not include the details. If this happens to you, continue to remind the counselee of the importance of immediate, clear goal setting, and perhaps help him or her form a concrete description. A vague description is usually expressed in generalizations and in empty or hard-to-define words. Always be on the lookout for the following vague phrases so that you can immediately communicate to your counselee that these types of phrases will only inhibit their goal setting, thus making it difficult for growth to occur. Many of these generalizations will sound familiar and can also be found in Dillon's book *Short-Term Counseling*.

1. *He always does that to me.* Rarely does anything happen "all the time." The generalization "always" defines the problem as continuous and gives the accused no credit when doing right.

2. *She expects me to read her mind.* "Expects" is difficult to define. What exactly does she do that tells you she has certain expectations?

3. *He never helps with the kids.* "Helping" with the kids is also vague. In what specific ways would she like him to help? Also, it is unlikely that he never helps.

4. *She never wants to have good sex.* When hearing this statement, I have no idea what the complaining spouse expects. What is the meaning of "good sex"? What would he like different?

5. *He's such a slob.* I have known some slobs in my life, but I do not know how this person is sloppy. How would he be different if he wasn't a slob?

6. *She expects too much of me.* Who can possibly know what is "expected" here? Specifically, what does she "expect" that is too much? How do you know she "expects" it?[6]

Fifth and last, one of the most important criteria in goal setting is the principle that each person can work toward achieving a goal themselves, regardless of what anyone else does. Spouses don't have to wait to change until the other changes. You may find one or both spouses resisting this idea, and it will be important to reemphasize that they are not dependent upon their spouses changing before they change.[7]

With the briefing on goal setting now introduced, it is time to move into the second most vital matter to the solution-focused approach—hypothetical solutions and exceptions.

Hypothetical Solutions and Exceptions

Do you recall the word "exceptions" used in the goal setting dialogue between the wife, husband and therapist? It is no coincidence that these two important concepts—hypothetical solutions and exceptions—follow in the footsteps of goal setting. Often these two concepts help an individual or couple gain clarity and draw closer to their personal goals. Let's first look at how you can point your counselees toward hypothetical solutions by using the following questions, taken from Walter and Peller's book *Becoming Solution-Focused in Brief Therapy*.

1. If something amazing happened overnight and you woke up tomorrow with your problem solved, what would you be doing differently?
2. Let's assume you are on track on how to approach your husband, so he responds to you. What do you see yourself doing differently?
3. When you feel accepted and loved, what will you have been doing?
4. When counseling is finished and it has been successful, what will you be doing differently? Or what will you be saying to yourself that is different?[8]

The following dialogue is between a counselor and his or her counselee, where the counselor implements questions similar to those above designed to help the counselee see the source of the problem differently, as well as recognize the ways he or she is changing.

> *Minister:* Jim, there have been times in the last 10 days when you have not had the typical problems you expected (*asking for exceptions*).
>
> *Jim:* I guess so. Actually, our relationship has been a bit better.
>
> *Minister:* What is it that you have been doing differently?
>
> *Jim:* I don't see much that I'm doing differently. Sheila has been better. She's not so defensive and she listens to me.
>
> *Minister:* You don't see yourself doing anything different?
>
> *Jim:* Not really, but she's changing.
>
> *Minister:* If I were talking with her, what might she say you've been doing differently?
>
> *Jim (Pauses.):* Probably nothing. I don't see myself being much different.
>
> *Minister:* From your perspective, Sheila is the one who is different. But let's consider how she might see this situation (*accepts the response but continues to ask the question*).
>
> *Jim:* Well, she might say I'm less belligerent and maybe I listen to her a bit more. I guess that's a possibility.
>
> *Minister:* So it's possible that with her changing maybe you are a bit different too (*considers another possibility*)?
>
> *Jim (Pauses.):* Yeah, I guess that's true. I am making some changes. Guess it's hard to admit.
>
> *Minister:* Jim, how did you decide to make those changes?
>
> *Jim:* I'm not sure; I guess it was conscious. Maybe it final-

ly dawned on me there had to be a better way. And you know, it could be that some of my changes encouraged Sheila.

Minister: That might be something for the two of you to talk about. This coming week consider the question, What do you see yourself doing differently *(uses several visual words to match Jim's style)*?

Jim: I hate to sound like a broken record, but Sheila really is the one doing more changing than I am. I think she'll continue to listen and be less defensive.

Minister: And when she is, how would she describe your responses?

Jim (Sighs.): Okay, okay. She'll say I'm more open and a better listener.

Minister: Like you are now?

Jim (Smiles.): Yes. You don't give up, do you?

Minister: Not when I see how you're changing and the potential you have.

By the minister responding to Jim in this manner, Jim eventually begins to see his spouse as less of the problem. The dialogue also encourages Jim's realization of his own contributions. You see, helping a counselee formulate a response draws them closer to accomplishing whatever goals were set.

As a counselor, you also need to learn how to help counselees find the exceptions or highlights in their marriages so that they can achieve their goals. What exactly is pointing out the exceptions? It's like this: A couple comes for counseling and focuses on the problems, ignoring the times when the problem isn't occurring, so you ask questions that help the counselee recognize the problem-free times. These problem-free times are what I call exceptions.

Be aware that the way a question is phrased can prevent a counselee from noting the exceptions. For example, if you ask, "Have there been times when this didn't occur?" you make it too easy for the counselee to respond with, "No, there haven't been any times." Instead, change your focus: "Tell me about the times when your wife is paying attention to you." "When are the times that the problem doesn't occur?" "I'd like to hear about the times when you are thinking positively about your husband. What happens then?"

Here is a verbatim exchange from a session I had with a couple who had been married for just eight months and both were fearful and concerned about becoming vulnerable when sharing their feelings.

Norm: So in the relationship you would be the one to give more information and perhaps talk more.

Sharon: I think, at times. Yes, at times I do.

Norm: Alright.

Sharon: There are times that I close off. I get kind of scared.

Norm: A little frightened?

Sharon: Yes.

Norm: What frightens you?

Sharon: That he won't understand. That he'll just go by it. It's like maybe I'll open myself a little, and then he won't see how sensitive it is for me or how important it is that he understand, and then that will make me close off again.

Norm: And you go back into your shell.

Sharon: Right.

Norm: Dennis, what's your perspective on the depth of communication and the concern you have? I'd like to hear that.

Dennis: Um, well, I think as a man that it's not natural for me to open up my deep feelings and thoughts. And though I want to be able to open up, it's not something that is easy for me. It's almost like I try to beat around the bush or I try to go about informing Sharon in other ways than just coming out and telling her I'm afraid of this situation happening right now. So often I feel that I need to have an answer and be in control as a man. And that would indirectly reassure me that I'm a good husband, a good provider and so forth. When I don't feel like things are together it's difficult for me, and then to come out and express myself, that isn't easy.

Norm: To admit that is really kind of scary.

Dennis: Right.

Norm: And so you would keep it inside and Sharon would go ahead and wonder, *Do you have any feelings? What's going on?* And she would feel sort of distant from you?

Dennis: Yes, and then I would fear rejection once I've exposed myself. It's like, okay, is she going to be receptive to it or is she going to perceive me as not being able to handle things or being weak and things of that nature?

Norm: Tell me about the times when you have gained the courage to open up and share.

Dennis: Well, I think you know as our relationship has progressed, we are learning more and more to communicate and our guard is—

Norm: Dropping?

Dennis: Dropping, and we do open up more and more as

time goes on.

Norm: So there are exceptions?

Dennis: Sure.

Norm: And the times that you have opened up, what has happened? Were you rejected or did she listen to you?

Dennis: No, I think for me it's almost been something I've built up like a façade that I'm afraid would drop if I exposed myself. When I've opened up, and though she may not always understand me or what I'm saying, she still didn't reject me. She was still there, and that in itself is a relief. And then as she observes me and watches how I am, she learns to understand me. She's a good observer.

Norm: So your fear of being rejected is really sort of unfounded because Sharon has not rejected you.

Dennis: Right.

Norm: And even though she doesn't fully understand, you're saying that's okay?

Dennis: Yes.

Norm: Sharon, what happens to you? How do you feel when Dennis does come to the place where he opens up?

Sharon: Real good.

Norm: Could you turn to Dennis and tell him?

Sharon (To Dennis.): I feel good but I'm still scared. I'm scared that I don't quite think I'm going to be able to handle it, understand or meet all your needs. I have a fear that I'll close up again because I just don't know how to handle it.

Norm: Have you ever said to him, "Gee, I appreciate you telling me about your feelings even though I'm not sure what to do with them at this point"? Have you ever said something like that?

Sharon: No. No, I haven't. I should say that, but—

Norm: Would that be an expression, though, of what you're feeling?

Sharon: Yes, it would. I feel too like if he opens up, I should have those right words to stroke him and say everything's okay, but sometimes I don't.

Norm: When you do share your feelings, what is it that you want to hear from Sharon? Could you tell her?

Dennis (To Sharon.): Just to reassure me that I'm okay, that you'll still stand by me even in times when I'm unsure, that you'll just be there by my side. I need you to reassure me that your world won't fall down when I think that our world, my world, is kind of in disarray, that my lacking won't cause you to be depleted.

Norm: How do you feel about that?

Sharon: It feels okay—safe.

Norm: Safe.

Sharon: Hmm.

Norm: That's something you could do?

Sharon: Yes, I could do that.

Norm: You're very articulate, Dennis.

Dennis: Thank you.

Norm: You might feel as though it is difficult for you to share, but the interchange just now showed me that you really have that capacity. There's a lot of depth there.

Do you see the importance of helping counselees pursue the exceptions? It helps couples become aware of the fact that they don't always struggle with problems and that it is possible to live in this different, positive way.[9] Exceptions are vital breaths to a marriage that affirm the couple in the good they are capable of doing.

Michele Weiner-Davis, author of *Divorce Busting*, describes this process of pointing out the exceptions in the following way:

> Notice what is different about the times the two of you are getting along. As you recall recent problem-free times or exceptions (there are almost always some of them), determine what *you* do differently during those times.
>
> If you are having difficulty answering this question, the following suggestion might help. Identify a recent peaceful time. For example, "Last night we had a reasonable conversation." Think carefully about what you were doing immediately preceding the conversation. Maybe you asked about your spouse's day or made a delicious dinner. Sometimes what you did differently preceding a peaceful time is subtle, so take your time thinking about it.
>
> Now, as a *result* of the "reasonable conversation," what were you more inclined to do that you hadn't been doing prior to it? In what ways did this conversation influence you to act differently? Perhaps you felt closer to your spouse and therefore initiated sex, or maybe, for the first time in weeks, you said good night as you went upstairs. Deciphering what you do immediately preceding and immediately following good times reveals what you must do to initiate and maintain desirable changes.[10]

When an exception is recognized, the old way of recalling only the problems is diminished because a new perspective exists. The new perspective shrinks rather than amplifies the problems. Exceptions also reveal to the couple that change and growth are possible. And by identifying an exception, it will help a person begin to look for and discover more exceptions, thus leading to the discovery of new solutions. Identifying an exception helps a person construct another exception to the problem, thus enabling the person to discover new solutions.

Michelle Weiner-Davis has also broached the subject of finding solutions in the exceptions in her book *Divorce Busting*. She takes on solution-oriented therapy and translates it into practical language and examples for the average person. Some of her suggestions are questions you can raise to assist the counseling couple in developing solutions. Here are some of the guidelines or questions to use:

1. What is different about the times you do get along? What are you doing? What are you saying?
2. What have you done in the last year that has made your marriage more fulfilling? Let's think about this together.
3. Let's talk about something you can accomplish this week—something that is possible.
4. Because you are still having many conflicts, I would like you to focus more on how your conflicts end. What brings them to a halt, who says and does what, etc.?
5. The next time this issue comes up I would like you to notice what's different about the times it's there but something constructive happens, or what's different about the times it's there but you're not bothered about what has happened.
6. This week I would like you to do something quite different. I would like you to sit down each night and predict whether the next day will be a good day or a bad day. Then at the end of the next day share together your

perception of that day, whether it went well or not. If you agreed that it did, put a checkmark on the calendar.[11]

For many couples this is effective. But why? How does this stop the negative behavior from continuing? One therapist describes the process this way:

> Prediction tasks are based on the idea that what you expect to happen is more likely to happen once the process leading up to it is in motion. In pragmatic terms, this means that the prediction, made the night before, can sometimes be seen as setting in motion the processes involved in having a better day. No matter what guess the predictor puts down, the idea that he might have a good day is bound to cross his mind. Of course, having a good day is what he really wants, and therefore a self-fulfilling prophecy might develop and this might prompt "better day behavior" the next day, right off the bat.[12]

Compliments and affirmations become a big part of the counseling process because you may be the only reinforcing person in their lives.

So there you have it—the solution-focused approach—the idea that concentrating on what works in a marriage helps a couple set goals, which in turn helps them notice the exceptions, which in turn helps them construct positive solutions. Pretty neat and simple, right? While it is a simple approach, it may take time for you to adapt to it if you have been practicing a different approach. Additionally, this approach expects a lot out of you, the counselor, but this is a good thing (notice the exception)! You become active in this process, rather than a passive observer.

The pastor's role is to be a cheerleader and encourage the person or couple about any changes and any problem solving they accomplish. Your expressed belief in their ability to change may be the power source they need for change to actually occur. Cheerleading is expressed through actual comments, gestures and other body language, the choice of phrases and words or tone of voice. Compliments and affirmations become a big part of the counseling process because you may be the only reinforcing person in their lives. We all need someone else to believe in us. Upon entering counseling, couples often feel deprived by their spouse of gratification, depleted in their reservoirs of what they can give and unappreciated for the efforts they expend. This can discourage anyone, so part of your role is to be an encourager so that the couple can begin finding the positives in their marriage.

Therefore encourage one another and build each other up, just as in fact you are doing (1 Thess. 5:11).

Sometimes cheerleading can be expressed through questions such as: "How were you able to do that?" "How do you think you were able to accomplish that in just a week's time? That's amazing!" Sometimes you will find the counselee discounting your positive observations or being amazed at what you are pointing out. Your role is to gently point out the positive that is occurring, and eventually you will see a change in their belief about themselves.

Let's close with an example of how your belief in a person can change his or her life. In *Chief*, the autobiography of former Los Angeles Police Chief Darryl Gates, he tells about his assignment as captain to the Highland Park precinct. An older lieutenant by the name of Harry had at one time been a great detective in the robbery division. But because of the use of excessive force in one case, he had been sent to Gates's division and put back on uniformed patrol.

When Captain Gates had his first meeting with his three lieutenants, Harry came in with a coffee cup and saucer and couldn't keep them still. They rattled as though a small earthquake were occurring, but it was just Harry shaking. He had all the visible signs of drinking too much, but at the time he was stone sober. He was merely nervous, and every time he came in contact with Captain Gates he had the same reaction. It occurred to Gates that Harry believed the captain had been sent there to get him and he was frightened to death. And nothing Captain Gates said to him reassured him.

At the time, a daytime burglar was creating havoc in the Highland Park precinct, committing three to four burglaries a day. Captain Gates called Harry in one day and told him he knew more about police work than all the other officers. He told Harry he wanted him to catch the burglar. If he could develop a plan, Gates knew it would work. Harry had a funny look on his face as he walked out.

Two days later Harry walked into Captain Gates's office to tell him the burglar had been caught. Gates just looked at him and told him he had never had a doubt in his mind that Harry could do it. He said Harry had done a fantastic job. He continued to praise Harry at every opportunity both privately and publicly. Harry seemed to change overnight. He stopped drinking and smoking. His appearance changed and he became the most attentive lieutenant Gates had. Harry's wife told Captain Gates she didn't know what he had done to Harry, but it had changed his life.

What Gates did was believe in Harry, in spite of past mistakes, and it turned Harry's life around.[13]

Why not make a goal for yourself today? Commit to at least try the solution-focused approach with one of your counselees in six sessions or less. Providing a positive outlook and perhaps a second chance for a troubled marriage could make all the difference. Look at Harry—could he have changed if someone wasn't in there encouraging him, pointing out he had what it took to get the job done?

Chapter 5

MAKE GOALS A REALITY

Session Two

Much of your effort in counseling is directed toward establishing goals with a couple in order to increase positive behavior in their marriage. Whatever is decided upon (usually in session one), the goals must receive significant attention so there is little chance of failure. A couple can increase positive behavior through several methods. Let's go ahead and explore a few.

CARING-DAYS

One successful method that increases positive behavior is a concept Dr. Richard Stuart calls "caring-days." I have used this concept in counseling and marriage seminars with scores of couples who have found it very helpful. I would like to highlight this method for you, so you can pass it on to couples when counseling.[1]

Before providing a full-blown explanation for the caring-days procedure, it is important for you to first think about three things. First, it is important to realize that the couple will be dealing with some conflicts that need a solution. You need to mention this challenge and point out that change must be undertaken as an orderly process. The first step in the process is developing the request for change and the simple behavior exchanges about to be described. Second, it is essential for you to stress that the initiation of the change process depends upon the willingness of both spouses to invest in relationship enhancement independently of the other—that what each spouse does is not dependent upon the other. Each spouse must act "as if" he or she cared for the other, if true caring is ever to be experienced. Generally, the spouse most willing to commit to change has the most to lose if the relationship does not improve. If this is the case, it may be better if you concentrate efforts on the other spouse, who is not as inclined to change. Hopefully your efforts will encourage the less-willing spouse to view the caring-days process as a low-cost method of discovering that the relationship can change. Remember, you can't proceed beyond

Love may or may not be the end point of counseling, but it cannot be its start.

this point without both spouses coming to at least hesitant agreement. Fortunately, factors such as the "halo" effect (when a person's overall impression of something or someone distorts his or her perceptions of specific qualities or actions) in the first session and a reasonable request should lead to agreement by both individuals, giving you one or two additional weeks of sessions needed for the couple to begin experiencing the benefits of this technique. It may help to ask each spouse to indicate on a scale from 0 to 10 both their willingness to change and then their belief about whether or not it will work. Finally, be sure you use the word "caring" and not "love." "Caring" is a very positive word that does not have as complex a meaning as "love." Couples are usually more willing to commit themselves to act as if they care for each other than to act as if they love one another. Love may or may not be the end point of counseling, but it cannot be its start.

Positive Requests

In caring-days each spouse is asked to answer the question, What would you like your spouse to do as a means of showing that he or she cares for you? Be specific. Answers to the question are written in the center column of a clean sheet of paper specially ruled for that purpose. The behaviors should meet the following criteria in order to be entered on the list:

- Positive
- Specific
- Small behaviors that can be done at least once daily
- Not the subject of a recent sharp conflict
- Inexpensive

Answers to the question that fit within the parameters are what I call requests. A positive request aims for an increase in positive behaviors, not a decrease in negative ones. "Please ask me how I spent my day" is a positive request that should be used in place of the negative request "Don't ignore me so much." A specific request is easily understood—"Come home at 6 P.M. for dinner"—which replaces the vague "Show more consideration for the family."

Why is this so important? Because small, potentially high-rate responses are needed at this stage of counseling if spouses are to enjoy the immediate changes that they need in order to gain confidence in the procedure, as well as in the remaining counseling sessions. Another example—"Please line the children's bikes along the back wall of the garage when you come home"—is a much more manageable request than "Please train the children to keep their bikes in the proper places." It is important to include relatively conflict-free requests on the caring-days list because neither spouse is likely to concede major points at this stage of counseling. As you adapt this procedure into your counseling sessions, you might find it interesting that some couples' conflict is actually a welcome response. Why? Many enjoy releasing energy and tension through anger, which unfortunately at times succeeds in immediate, short-lived change in the nonaggressor's behavior. This is a dangerous game to play, as couples in this type of situation will likely hold on to these short-lived benefits, or good times, instead of developing trust for the long run, a time that might seem far off but that when invested in, can expect longer-range reciprocation of the positives.

Manageable Lists

While it is typical for a couple to begin listing requests that are negative, vague and perhaps full of conflict, it is your responsibility to help them construct positive request lists. You can show them some acceptable examples. It is also appropriate for you to help construct the spouses' responses and edit requests before they are written on the list. The couple should also be encouraged to not only brainstorm and add during the session but also to do so during the week between sessions. The list should include at least 15 to 18 items for several important reasons. First, the items are contributed by both spouses, and some have greater importance to one spouse than to the other. Second, some of the items will seem much more relevant and feasible on some days, thus providing the opportunity to express caring and commitment freely, while on other days it will seem like pulling teeth. To avoid this inconsistency, help the counselees think about various alternatives that will help to overcome any feelings of monotony in their daily request exchange. Finally, interests shift over time, so keeping the list between 15 and 18 allows for an open-ended list that can keep pace with changes in one or both spouses' preferences. Remember, coaching a couple initially to select 15 to 18 items and then continue adding several items to the list each week builds an effective list with sufficient breadth and responsiveness.

Forward Progress

When the list has been completed, each request should be discussed. The spouse making the request should state precisely what, when and how he or she would like the other to respond. Encourage each spouse to share his or her request with an appropriate tone of voice. The spouse listening to the request should ask for clarification about any ambiguities during the session.

Then each spouse should be asked to make a commitment to do at least five of the behaviors on the caring-days list daily. Five a day will provide frequent demonstrations of each spouse's willingness to meet their spouse's expectations. Moreover, each spouse should make positive investments in improving the marriage relationship regardless of whether or not the other has made similar gestures. This condition is important, because spouses in distressed marriages tend to inhibit positive interaction through their reliance upon what is called the change-second principle. According to this principle, each person decides that he or she will act positively only after the other has offered a positive behavior. Does this sound familiar? The problem is that as each spouse awaits a positive behavior from the other, neither spouse ever takes the constructive steps that are needed to improve their relationship. It is a standoff. Therefore, the caring-days procedure asks each spouse to agree to the change-first principle, saying that they expect to change before the other, which sets the process of change in motion.

In addition to taking frequent, independent action, each should be encouraged to record his or her progress on the list. Next to whatever request each spouse has received from the other, it is important they make note of the progress and include the date it occurred. For example, the husband enters the date beside the behaviors completed by his wife under a column titled "Wife," while the wife does the same thing under the column titled "Husband." These written records serve several functions that help a couple determine if progress was made or not. For example, distressed couples tend to take for granted the positives that are offered to one another. Written acknowledgment of these events helps verify that positives really do occur and helps each person identify the behaviors that may have been overlooked. In addition, the record serves as a visual reminder of the amount of change that has taken place. This is an excellent way of overcoming the pessimism that hampers many couples' belief in the possibility that their marriage can improve. Finally, the record is a source of data for use in evaluating the willingness of both spouses to take constructive, assertive action in response to therapeutic instigations.

CARING-DAYS SAMPLE LISTS

I realize that some of you might be visual learners, like me, so I have included sample caring-days lists from both a husband and wife. Feel free to adapt from the lists and create your own sample lists for counselees.

Wife's Caring-Days List

1. Greet me with a kiss and hug in the morning before we get out of bed.
2. Bring me pussy willows (or some such).
3. Ask me what music I would like to hear and put it on.
4. Reach over and touch me when we're riding in the car.
5. Make me breakfast and serve it to me.
6. Tell me you love me.
7. Put your things away when you come in.
8. It you're going to stop at the store for something, ask me if there is anything that I want or need.
9. Rub my body or some part of me before going to sleep, with full concentration.
10. Look at me intently sometimes when I'm telling you something.
11. Engage actively in fantasy trips with me.
12. Ask my opinions about things that you write and let me know which suggestions you follow.
13. Tell me when I look attractive.
14. Ask me what I'd like to do for a day or weekend with the desire to do what I suggest.

Husband's Caring-Days List

1. Wash my back.
2. Smile and say you're glad to see me when you wake up.

3. Fix the orange juice.
4. Call me at work.
5. Acknowledge my affectionate advances.
6. Invite me to expose the details of my work.
7. Massage my shoulders and back.
8. Touch me while I drive.
9. Hold me when you see that I'm down.
10. Tell me about your experiences at work every day.
11. Tell me that you care.
12. Tell me that I'm nice to be around.[2]

Increasing these behaviors is a practical application of the biblical principles that tell us to love and care for another person (see 1 Cor. 13:4-8). The caring-days approach is based upon the mutual cooperation of the couple. Some counselors have found it beneficial to explore with the couple what may occur if one of them fails to follow through on fulfilling their spouse's requests. Try to convey to a couple that whenever a failure occurs, discouragement will follow. Heeding this notice, a couple might avoid a situation where one or both spouses sabotage the approach by not following through, thus lessening the possibility of failure.

GUIDELINES THAT WORK

Share with a couple the following list of guidelines that reveal how to move into a positive way of thinking and way of life. These really do work.

Go out of Your Way
First, whenever time has been spent apart from one another—even briefly (perhaps a few hours)—greet one another with a

smile and a genuine compliment. Share a positive or interesting incident. Ask questions that will cause your spouse to want to share more information.

Open Up the Lines of Communication

Second, make use of "transition times," periods of time between leaving work (or other stressful activities) and returning home. Take the time to diffuse any frustrations, fears, pressures or problems of the day. Doing this lessens the possibility of such factors affecting the marital communication.

Know When to Turn Talk Off

Third, avoid discussing important topics that have disagreement potential when either spouse is emotionally or physically exhausted, ill, in pain or medicated.

Set a Time for "Problem Talks"

Fourth, consider establishing a set time each day for items that involve decision making, problem solving, and conflict or business resolution. For a couple to succeed in setting aside time for these issues, they must commit themselves to a "No interruptions and no use of this time for other activities" rule. Additionally, whether the couple has a set time for discussion or not, it is important for them to understand and agree to the following communication concepts:

1. It is best to discuss complaints, joint decisions and disagreements during an agreed-upon decision-making time.
2. It is important to remain on a topic until each person has had an opportunity to share his or her thoughts or feelings.

3. Discussions of controversial issues and problems should focus upon the present. (Often counselors may give couples a specific directive not to discuss the past or debate what may occur in the future.)

4. Specific, clear statements are more effective than generalizations and overstatements. Accuracy in description will help keep the communication progressing smoothly.

5. When one spouse is talking, the other is to give total attention. Verbal responses showing that the person is in tune with the spouse assists the process and proves that the person is really listening.

6. All mind reading and speaking for the other person must be avoided.

7. Debating over trivial or insignificant details is to be avoided.

8. If you have difficulty understanding what your spouse said or meant, repeat what you think he or she said and meant. Then ask, "Is this accurate?"

9. Whenever your spouse communicates in a manner you desire, praise and reinforce your spouse for what he or she has done.

10. Each person needs the freedom to discuss topics he or she enjoys or those of importance to him or her. However, each person also needs to discuss topics that interest the other, communicating in a way that pleases the other. This enhances the relationship.

11. All labeling should be avoided. Words such as "lazy," "inconsiderate," "stubborn," "intolerant" and "cruel" will only create more difficulty.

12. "Why" questions are not problem-solving questions. They are directed toward the cause, rather than the

solution. Questions such as, Why did this happen? or Why did you do that? usually make a person feel threatened or defensive, or will cause the person to wonder if he or she is being criticized.

13. It is important to understand that human messages consist of three components: 7 percent content, 38 percent tone of voice and 55 percent nonverbal (or body language). These three figures need to be consistent or confusion will emerge between spouses. For example, frowning or scowling when giving a compliment confuses the recipient. Therefore, couples should give attention to tone of voice and nonverbal components of their communication. (Videotaping a couple's communication during the counseling sessions will enlighten them about these processes more than any other means.)

14. When a problem is presented, begin with something positive. The initial presentation of a problem sets the tone for further discussion. Two common difficulties with problem presentation is that the statements are general and negative. The best approach is to begin with a positive statement, if possible, and then make the request specific and positive. Point to the behavior you desire from the other person. The praise is not to be invented but genuine. The counselor should have the couple consider what it is they want from each other when they pose a problem or lodge a complaint: Is it anger, defensiveness or resistance toward the other person? Or openness, cooperation and a change for the other person? The way the spouse approaches a problem will determine the response.

For example, a spouse can approach a situation by complaining. Here are two examples of typical complaints: "You are not involved enough with the children" and "You are never affectionate." On the other hand, the spouse could easily rephrase the comment into positive language and say: "I appreciate your evaluating your schedule so you could spend more time with us" and "I enjoy when you touch me. I would appreciate it if you would touch me and hold me several times a day and also let me know if you like something I'm doing." Recognition and praise are positive ways to express to your spouse that he or she is worthy and special.

MORE GUIDELINES THAT WORK

Recognition and praise also open the door for people to begin accepting things about themselves they need to change—what I deem constructive suggestions—in order to have a better marriage.

On occasion, a spouse might attempt a constructive suggestion by asking a clarifying question or even a defensive question to his or her spouse. It is important for the questioned spouse to answer with a straight, positive response:

> *Question:* "I spend enough time with the kids. What's the problem?"
>
> *Response:* "In the last two weeks you spent time with them on three evenings. We are saying we want more of you than that."

Do you see how the questioned spouse responded to the loaded question? Because of the calm, straightforward approach, the spouse was able to answer the question without adding insult to injury, thus diminishing the possibility of a heated discussion or argument.

Another complaint was registered concerning picking up after himself around the home, and it was defensively challenged. A specific answer needs to follow. "Today you left the dishes on the table, the newspaper on the floor in the family room and a coffee cup on the good table. I would appreciate it if you would . . . "

Using this positive approach, couples need to learn seven additional skills.

1. Talking to Each Other

Because a major emphasis of behavioral marital counseling is to alter the interaction style of the couple, most of the therapy session is spent with the spouses talking to each other and not to the therapist. This emphasis also helps to reduce or eliminate the tendency of many spouses to draw the therapist onto "their side," against their mate.

2. Making Eye Contact

Eye contact is encouraged because it can form a bond that helps the spouses work together as a team. Averted eyes may indicate a distracted or uninterested spouse, and this may lead to resentful feelings.

3. Making "I" Statements

These statements usually start with "I feel" or "I think" and take the place of statements that speak about or for the spouse ("You feel" or "You think"). These statements provide direct information about the person's own feelings and encourage the spouses to take responsibility for their behavior and feelings. Remember that non-verbal behavior accounts for 55 percent of one verbalized message.

4. Practicing Reflective Listening

Reflective listening shows that the spouse is listening to and understanding what the speaker is saying rather than day-dreaming or planning rebuttals. This skill is especially helpful for couples who frequently interrupt each other, because it slows down their pace of interaction and teaches them to listen to each other.

5. Giving Praise

In order to change the couple's negative reinforcement schedule to a positive one, couples should be encouraged to give positive reinforcement directly. They should be encouraged to tell each other what he or she likes about the spouse, what the spouse has been doing well and what the spouse says that is helpful.

6. Giving Head Nods

Although they can lose effectiveness if overdone, head nods are a good communication skill because they are a nonverbal way of telling the speaker that his or her message is being received.

7. Stating What the Person Likes or Wants

In the problem-solving format, the therapist provides a safe situation in which spouses may honestly state what they like and want. Thus, they can be encouraged to be open about their wants.[3]

As you can see, session two moves a couple beyond goal-setting and gets them to take action. By committing to procedures and methods that will breed positive interaction, couples will achieve their goals, thus leading to a happier marriage. As we move on to session three, you will continue to see different ways in which negative behaviors are broken and positive behaviors reinforced.

Chapter 6

CHANGE THE OUTLOOK

Session Three

As you progress through sessions one and two with a couple, you will begin to recognize behavioral patterns and habits the couple has perhaps lived with since first dating. Whatever their situation, the couple needs you to continue helping them reach their goals by breaking free from negativity. To do this, you will need to devote at least one session to working with the inner cognition or thoughts of a couple. Basically, you need to help the couple discover the values they attribute to behaviors, which tend to communicate their thoughts about a relationship.

DEFINE SENDER'S AND RECEIVER'S RULES

Sometimes I refer to thoughts as sender's rules and receiver's rules. A sender's rule is a thought such as, *If I love and care for you, I will show it by this behavior* or *I'll do this; it is an indication that I love you.*

The person on the other end, the receiver, then has the thought, *If you love me, I will know it by seeing you do this behavior*. Another receiver response is, *If you do this behavior, it is an indication that you love and value me*. When these value thoughts, messages and behaviors correspond with each other, the relationship will experience fewer problems.

Difficulties arise for couples when the receiver's rule for a value message does not correspond to the sender's rule. For purposes of illustration, let's say the wife is the receiver and the husband is the sender. In this case, she does not get the value message but not because he is purposely trying to send a message of no value. It is because their language or style of communication is different (see chapter 3).

Clarify the Meaning of Behavior

One of the first steps that needs to occur for the couple to understand each other's value messages is to clarify their meanings of behavior. And surprise, surprise: Clarifying a couple's behavior is the job of the counselor or minister. Through clarification, the husband and wife can change the thoughts of the sender, the thoughts of the receiver or both. And again, clarification comes when a couple realizes they have different styles of communication and therefore need to adapt to one another's preferences and senses. As soon as a couple knows this, they usually feel a sense of relief that the solution is not all that difficult and threatening.

I bet you would like to see a "clarifying of behaviors" in action. Here is one example of a husband who is irritated about some of his wife's behaviors. He feels he has been slighted a number of times. One of his main complaints is that she is frequently late for appointments they have together. The question their counselor needs to consider is, What does this behavior on the part of the wife mean to the husband? The husband's thoughts are, *If she really loved me, she wouldn't be late.* What creates the conflict is not necessarily that the husband feels this way but that what the husband means by being late is not the same as what the wife thinks about being late. Although she knows he dislikes her being late, she doesn't equate promptness with her loving or caring for him. Her family simply never put a priority on being on time, so promptness is not a priority for her. On the other hand, the husband came from a family where lateness had a more significant meaning, such as not caring. Therefore, his mind-set was, *If you love me, you'll be on time.* As you can see, the wife's mind-set does not correspond with her husband's values; therefore, their behaviors toward promptness are extremely different.

How can couples break out of this binding pattern? Several possibilities are available to you. Here is one: If the wife realizes the significance of being on time (meaning it will show her husband that she loves and cares for him), she will have a good reason to change her pattern of tardiness. Here is another: If the husband begins to alter his thought life or value system concerning the idea that tardiness does not mean his wife doesn't care, he opens himself up to accepting a new belief or value that corresponds with his wife's value system. To incorporate this sort of change, the husband needs to rehearse over and over again in his head that her lateness does not mean she does not love him and that she has her own reasons for being late, which stem from her upbringing. He could also think other good thoughts: *I don't care for her being late, but that doesn't mean she doesn't care for me. I will find other indications that she loves me.*

For further understanding, let's take a look at another example. A husband attempts to demonstrate his love for his family by working long hours in order to provide for them. His mind-set is, *I demonstrate my love by working hard.* However, his wife does not see it that way. Her value message is, *Why does he spend so much time at work? If he really loved me, he would be here with me and the children!* He feels devalued by her lack of response to his love. The question their counselor needs to consider is, What does this behavior on the part of the husband mean to the wife? So the first question the counselor needs to ask to the husband is what his expectations are concerning displays of appreciation. Perhaps he would indicate that he expects her to be grateful for his faithful provider role, and that he should be receiving thanks, not criticisms, for his sacrifices.

On the flip side, she does not think, *I love you; therefore I appreciate your working,* but instead, *I love you; therefore I want you with me more. So I'll try to have you with me no matter what I have to do.* Her want for this togetherness may invoke responses of anger, complaining, nagging, crying or other behaviors that turn the husband away. Do you see how the wife's responses could create confusion for the husband? What she wants—to be together—she is ironically pushing away because her husband only senses her negative behaviors. And why would the husband think the wife wanted to be together if she was constantly responding negatively? Here are four possible suggestions from Dr. Joseph Strayhorn that would change this relationship:

1. He can cut down on how much he works.
2. She can change her view of his working so hard.
3. She can show appreciation for his sacrifice.
4. He can change his view of her absence of appreciation.
   Any one of these changes will help the relationship.[1]

As you work with a couple, it is important to help them discover the following:

- What behaviors does your spouse perform that indicate he or she loves you?
- What behaviors does your spouse need to perform to indicate he or she loves you?

A great resource that will help you through the behavior-values process is *The Marriage Checkup Questionnaire*, which provides couples an opportunity to reflect on and answer questions such as, What five behaviors or tasks does your spouse do that you appreciate? and, What four important requests do you have for your spouse at this time?[2]

Clarify the Options for Changing Behavior

When working with a couple experiencing miscommunication, counselors must help them understand the specific miscommunication. This involves clarifying the meaning attached to the behavior in question. From what you just read, the counselor or minister assumes the role of diplomat and helps the couple realize that perhaps their two different value systems don't add up. Once clarified, the value systems need to be altered from one or both spouses so that the couple understands one another.

The next step involves clarifying the options available to each person. Rather than the minister or counselor telling the couple what thoughts to change, it is better for the couple to make the decision and state specifically the ways they would like to change their thoughts and behaviors.

A common resistance you will encounter when couples begin clarifying how they would like to change values and behaviors is a new expectation. Listen to one husband's expectation: *Now that I've clarified for my spouse what my behavior (such as working long hours) means, she should just accept the condition.* Her clarification on the other hand says: *His working long hours does not convey love and also causes me to think he doesn't want to be around; he should cut down on time spent at work.* In the case of new expectations, both spouses should be asked how they can change their own thoughts and behaviors, not how the other can change.

Assist the couple in learning how to develop new thought patterns and visualize new positive behaviors they can do for each other.

From here, counselors need to assist the couple in learning how to develop new thought patterns and visualize new positive behaviors they can do for each other. This needs to be done prior to a new expectation occurring for three reasons. First, the emotion accompanying a new expectation is so strong, it becomes difficult to develop constructive patterns of response, which the individual needs to construct before the negative emotions kick in. Clear thinking is shut down because of physiological changes. Second, by visualizing and rehearsing new behavioral and thought responses in advance, the individual has committed to a plan for positive change. Third, it is important to be rooted in positive thought patterns so as not to let a new expectation concern the individual to the point that he or she is purposely continuing the negative behavior.

Let's take a closer look at how reason three can be handled. One way is to tell the couple that occasionally when couples clarify their thoughts to each other, one or both spouses may try to use this clarification in a negative manner. For example, a husband gets angry at his wife for assuming he doesn't love her because of the long hours he works. So he decides not to express his anger directly. Instead, he continues to work long hours, even though he knows this upsets his wife, making her feel devalued. At this point he cannot say he didn't know what this meant to her. The fact is he did know and chose to continue out of anger a behavior he knew was mismatched with his wife's values. On the other hand, if the wife began to tolerate his long hours and accept the fact that this didn't mean he devalued her, then his attempt to use his long hours to express anger is not going to succeed.

Using this example to illustrate how we can sometimes mis-use new information may stop a problem from occurring before it ever has a chance to start. To continue a clarified behavior after both spouses know how it affects the other and what it means to the other usually represents an act of hostility.[3] Since your goal is to be sure new behavior and thought responses are working, review at the next session what positive changes occurred in between sessions.

TAKE IT IN STAGES

As you proceed through this session with the couple, you will need to take the behaviors-values process in stages.

Stage One

Starting this process is usually the most difficult, as couples need to first acknowledge that they have different styles of com-munication that affect their beliefs, which in turn affect their behaviors. Be sure to begin your questioning by having each per-son share the reason their own behaviors (the ones that are caus-ing problems) are so important to them. Also ask them to share their value message for each behavior to their spouse.

Stage Two

As the couple acknowledges their differences, ask each person if he or she is aware of how the spouse would like this behavior performed based on his or her values. If the person doesn't know, have him or her ask the spouse to provide the information. (This is a great opportunity to demonstrate for the couple how responses can be shared in a positive manner.) Here is a series of questions you can ask each spouse about the other's conflicting behavior:

1. What is the value message you hear regarding your spouse's behavior?
2. Would you put this into words for me?
3. Do you think your spouse believes the same as you do about this behavior?
4. Do you think the same value message exists? What do you think he or she believes about this behavior?

Stage Three

As you now work through the last stage, reverse the process I have been describing. For example, as you read what each person thinks his or her spouse would like him or her to do more often, ask, "I wonder what your spouse's value message is concerning that behavior? What do you feel about this behavior and what does it mean to you?" The idea here is to get them to immediately look at a problem not as a problem but just as a differing behavior value. This will create less tension and give the couple the confidence that their lives aren't riddled with conflict.

ENCOURAGE SUCCESS

Dr. Everett Worthington, Jr., and Douglas McMurray have stated that if negative thinking isn't changed by both spouses, changes made in counseling probably won't last. They suggest that couples need their thoughts changed in four areas before success can occur.

Negative Thinking About the Marriage

Couples who come to you for counseling will probably bring with them negative and pessimistic thoughts about their marriage. These thoughts have built their negative feelings about one another and their relationship. Your task will be to teach them how to recognize these thoughts, interpret them and replace them with realistic and positive uplifting thoughts about their spouses.

Attributions That Blame Their Spouse

To break the pattern of blame, assist each spouse to see the issue from the other spouse's perspective. It is interesting to have one spouse attempt to describe what he or she thinks the other spouse is thinking and feeling, and then check it out with the spouse. Each spouse needs to be encouraged to take responsibility for solving the problem, rather than blaming. Spouses asking "What would you do?" can be helpful. This question attempts to replace the blame with empathy.

Expectations About the Future of Their Marriage

Expectations can also build poor behavior-values communication if troubled couples expect their marriages to continue in a negative way. This is where you can generate hope—by having couples identify times when their relationship was positive and discovering what they did to make that happen. Ask some questions: "What might happen if you responded that way again?" "What will it take for you to change things to be like that again?" "What can you do differently to make your marriage fulfilling now?" It is important to turn a couple's thoughts to the hope of Scripture as well. Share with the couple the following verses and ask them how they can apply these to their marriage.

> Call to Me and I will answer you and show you great and mighty things, fenced in and hidden, which you do not know (do not distinguish and recognize, have knowledge of and understand) (Jer. 33:3, *AMP*).

> For I know the plans I have for you, says the Lord. They are plans for good and not for evil, to give you a future and a hope. In those days when you pray, I will listen (Jer. 29:11-12, *TLB*).

Assumptions About the Marriage Itself

The final area in overcoming negative thoughts is to change assumptions about the marriage. These are not always easy to identify, but they definitely influence how a person behaves. Here are some common assumptions from Worthington and McMurray:

1. To demonstrate love, my husband must tell me he loves me several times daily.
2. If I don't feel romantic with my wife, it means we aren't in love any longer.
3. My husband should meet all my needs, especially all my needs for intimacy.
4. My wife should support all my ideas or else she doesn't love me.
5. When I've had a bad day, my husband should be able to sense it and should do something to cheer me up without my having to tell him.

6. My wife should not expect me to be courteous and polite to her. That's what marriage is all about—being yourself and not having to put on some show.

7. My husband should be able to know how to stimulate me when we're making love. I shouldn't have to tell him what to do and when to do it.

8. My wife and I should do almost everything as a couple if we are to maintain a happy marriage.

9. I should be able to keep my spouse from ever getting unhappy.

10. My wife and I should never argue or disagree if our marriage is good.[4]

These sample assumptions can destroy marriages. Therefore, Dr. Worthington and Pastor McMurray suggest the following five steps to avoid destructive assumptions:

1. Help the couple become aware that much of the way they behave is fashioned by their thoughts or assumptions. Share with the couple the above list and explain why these can create marital discord.

2. Help them identify the assumptions they have about their own marriage. You could ask, "What are the thoughts or assumptions you hold about marriage?" When each one has shared, ask, "How do you know that assumption is true? Where is the evidence for this belief?"

3. Explore the consequences of each of their assumptions. Discuss how each one affects their behavior. This could encourage them to change. I often ask, "If this weren't true or you didn't believe this, how might you behave differently?"

4. Help each one change the assumptions they want to change. Teach them how to challenge each one.

5. Provide the couple with examples of others who dealt with a similar assumption. You can accomplish this through other couples' interviews or through written resources. This step usually makes it easier for the couple to change their own assumptions.[5]

TEACH KIND WORDS

Another approach I use is to ask each person to indicate two or three areas of conflict where they seem to be at a deadlock. Impasse usually occurs because each spouse has a different belief or value about the behavior. Using the behavior-values procedure, the counselor and the couple explore the conflict areas together.

Yet another approach is to ask each person to write a list of behaviors that convey a love response. Ask each person to make a list starting with the heading, "I feel it is a sign of love if you . . . " or "I feel that if you love me you will . . . " Here is an example of one such list:

I feel it is a sign of love if you . . .

1. say "I love you."
2. say other things more or less synonymous with "I love you" (e.g., "I'm so glad we're together" or "You make me feel wonderful").
3. express your intention to stay in the relationship.
4. make me or buy me presents.
5. show me appreciation and gratitude for the things I do for you.

6. compliment me on things I did that you like or ways I am that you like.
7. remember special occasions such as birthdays or anniversaries.
8. touch me in a loving way.
9. say things to other people that cast me in a favorable light.
10. seem to enjoy sexual activity with me.
11. smile, brighten up and look happy when you have me around (i.e., communicate nonverbally "I'm happy you're around").
12. look for recreational activities for us to do together.
13. are interested when I talk about my experiences and my feelings.
14. disclose things to me about yourself, your experiences and your feelings.
15. dress or attend to personal hygiene in a way you know I like.
16. help me do chores and jobs.
17. laugh at things I do or say that are meant to be funny.
18. make up little surprises for me—leave notes for me that express positive feelings, make up poems for me, stop by unexpectedly and do things that let me know you're thinking about me when I wasn't expecting you to be.
19. are willing to talk about the relationship, think about ways to improve it and talk about things you or I can do to make either or both of us happier with the relationship.
20. give in and sacrifice a certain fraction of time when our wishes conflict, assuming that I'm also willing to give in and sacrifice part of the time.
21. play and act silly with me.

Get the couples you counsel on the right track. Whether or not you have them create love lists, the idea is to help them succeed in the behavior-values process. Tell them that when they renew

Marital counseling is designed to allow the couple to mature spiritually in both thought life and behaviors.

their minds and overcome negative thoughts, that is when behavioral changes can occur. Why not suggest to the couple to tack the following verse onto their bathroom mirror or refrigerator door—somewhere that they will see it often?

> Do not conform any longer to the pattern of this world, but be transformed by the renewing of your mind. Then you will be able to test and approve what God's will is— his good, pleasing and perfect will (Rom. 12:2).

You see, marital counseling is designed to allow the couple to mature spiritually in both thought life and behaviors. Such spiritual maturity will bring greater stability to their emotional life as well as to their marriage. And couples will experience a higher level of spiritual maturity when they overcome negative mind-sets, allowing them to meet one another's needs.

Chapter 7

MEET IN THE MIDDLE

Session Four

The needs of every man and woman vary, but some are quite predictable. It is your job in this session to have couples acknowledge their own needs as well as what they think their spouse's needs are. Dr. Willard Harley, Jr., has identified five basic needs men expect their wives to fulfill and five basic needs wives expect their husbands to fulfill. Of course, exceptions to these exist, but overall the majority of couples from his experiences fit this pattern.

A Man's Five Most Basic Needs

1. Sexual fulfillment
2. Recreational companionship
3. An attractive spouse
4. Domestic support
5. Admiration

A Woman's Five Most Basic Needs

1. Affection
2. Conversation
3. Honesty and openness
4. Financial support
5. Family commitment[1]

Often these needs go unmet, and when they are unmet, people often look outside the marriage for fulfillment. This is when a lot of problems tend to occur.

OPEN A LOVE ACCOUNT

To avoid the pitfalls of seeking fulfillment outside of marriage, it is important to create a healthy, positive, communicative relationship. Several therapists have developed an approach to increase pleasurable interaction based upon the concept of a bank account. Dr. Harley describes it as a "Love Bank." Every time a spouse interacts with their spouse they either make a deposit or a withdrawal. A pleasurable interaction is a deposit and a painful one is a withdrawal. Some couples create huge deposits whereas others operate in the red. When couples meet each other's most important needs, the love units deposited generate romantic love.[2]

Learn the Rules

The authors of *We Can Work It Out* have a model they call the relationship bank account. In it, a deposit can be anything from a small act of kindness to a large gesture of love and affection. Withdrawals can also be large or small and include anything negative or destructive. Even rudeness is a withdrawal! When

couples become aware of this concept, they learn how to identify attempted deposits and avoid withdrawals in order to develop
a healthy balance. Additionally, strong reserves are needed to
sustain the difficult times in a marriage. (The authors also suggest the value of the deposit or withdrawal be set by the receiving spouse, or the "teller.")

Additionally, the greater the balance, the easier it is to handle a withdrawal. But if a balance hovers around zero, a small
withdrawal has a great impact. And because of differences in
communication styles, if a couple does not learn to speak one
another's language and then the spouses attempt to make
deposits in their style, not their spouse's style, this might be
interpreted as a withdrawal by the spouse! Conversely, spouses
who understand and adapt to each other's styles make deposits.[3]

Make More Deposits
It is important for the couples you work with to know that one
negative comment or act can erase 20 positive acts. This is why
you need to stress that the first four minutes of the day, the last
four minutes before a couple separates for the day and the first
four minutes at the end of the workday are critical times and
need to be filled with positives, affirmations, concern for the
other and touching. These are massive deposits that set a positive tone for what occurs over the next few hours.[4]

SHARE YOUR NEEDS

The relationship bank account is a great way to keep track of
how couples meet each other's needs. However, before spouses
can meet needs, they need to know what those needs are. People
cannot read minds, and when they are expected to do so, it is not
only frustrating but also a total impossibility! In marital coun-

seling, a great way to have couples share their needs is to ask each person to specifically define those needs, to describe how the spouse can meet them and then share them with each other.

What to Share

Here is an example from my book *The Pillars of Marriage* of how one woman in premarital counseling shared her needs and how she thought her future husband could specifically meet them:

My Emotional Needs	How My Spouse Can Meet Them
To feel loved, cherished	Call me, prepare me for sex, hold me, kiss me, look at me with a glimmer in your eye, take naps so you will feel refreshed to be with me.
To feel supported, believed in	Pray for me in front of me and privately as well. Challenge me, praise me, see my potential in specific situations.
To feel comforted when down	Hold me, let me cry on your shoulder, feel my hurt with me, be gentle and sensitive to my moods, let me know you notice them.
To feel not alone	Share my daily joys and sorrows, enter into the conversation

about my day, be interested in daily details that help you understand me.

| To feel free to be myself | Be yourself, be genuine, see through my masks and let me know it. Know that I love you deep down so you can take my present anger. Accept my goofy antics as me, but when you don't like them, let me know gently what you prefer instead and give me the opportunity to change it. |

My Social Needs	How My Spouse Can Meet Them
To get together with other women	Encourage me to get to know friends and neighbors when I feel timid, and ask me what I learned afterward.
To get together as a couple	Be yourself, laugh at yourself, at me, at us, with friends and share it with others. Be as uninhibited as you dare.
To do something spontaneous	Go out to dinner, movies, a friend's house, miniature golf, something new—surprise me!

To get away from the house	Notice when I am useless and suggest a change of pace, just like when you feel cooped up and need a change.[5]

Lists created by couples are a first step in learning how to openly share about each other's needs. Lists also help when one or both spouses have difficulty expressing their needs.

When to Share
Couples need to share their initial requests of one another in the presence of the counselor, so he or she has an opportunity to evaluate and comment on the mode in which the counselees

Requesting needs should be made by giving a positive indication of what is desired.

send their messages. The use of a tape recorder or a video recorder has proven to be a great help in showing an individual or couple how they communicate, which they are unaware of a lot of the time.

How to Share
Requesting needs should be made by giving a positive indication of what is desired. There must be no criticism or reference to the past. The counselor might suggest prefacing requests with

statements such as "I would like you to" or "I would really appreciate it if you would."

Requests should only include those behaviors that are somewhat easy for the spouse to perform. And any central or main issue that brought the couple in for counseling should not be the substance of the request at this time.

It is probably obvious to us as counselors that when a positive behavior is performed toward another person, it should be positively reinforced. But such awareness is not always obvious to a counseling couple, so it needs to be explained to the counselees through examples and illustrations. Encourage couples to read the book *His Needs, Her Needs* by Dr. Willard F. Harley, Jr., for an expansion of these concepts.[6]

Sometimes one or both spouses will object to expressing needs to the spouse, so it is important to be aware of common problems and to know how to answer the objections. Three statements typify reactions a counselor might hear. These statements might also give an insight into previous occurrences between the couple in their day-to-day life.

1. Expecting spouse to be a mind reader: "Why should I tell him? We've been married for 10 years and he ought to know what I want."

Even if it were possible for one spouse to read the other's mind, 100 percent accuracy would be unlikely. It frustrates the spouse and places unrealistic demands on his or her ability to perform.

2. Not giving spouse the benefit of the doubt: "The only reason he's going to do this is because of your recommendation. He doesn't really want to. That's hypocritical."

Even if the person performing the positive behavior is hesitant and not fully committed, at least he or she is willing to try to see what improvements may occur. I often say, "At least your spouse is willing to follow my suggestions. I know many who won't."

3. Spouse's lack of belief: "It won't do much good to tell her. She's been aware for some time but has never responded. Why now?"

This lack of belief in the spouse's ability to change or to mature presents a definite roadblock to the future of the marriage. It is highly discouraging to the spouse who believes it can work. This is a time to move the objecting spouse to the point of belief by countering his or her attitude gently.

Responding to this lack of belief can be done in several ways. It is important here, as with other reactions, to value and respect the person's perspective of the relationship. Preface each comment with "I can understand your hesitancy based upon your present feelings" and then move to whatever response you plan to make. Here are some examples of responses for the counselor:

1. "Let's explore the future, say, the next two or three months. If we don't believe John will be any different, what will it be like?"
2. "I'm wondering what John is feeling right now as he's sitting here listening to us. Would you like to hear from him?"
3. "John, could you share with your wife your feelings about what she has said?"
4. "I get the impression from what you shared with me earlier that you have a concern for a biblical model of

marriage. Could I direct you to 1 Corinthians 13:7
(*AMP*) that might assist you in achieving that goal?
'Love bears up under anything and everything that
comes, is ever ready to believe the best of every person, its hopes are fadeless under all circumstances,
and it endures everything [without weakening].'
How would this passage give us a basis for the marriage you seek? How could this passage be applied?"

The thought expressed in 1 Corinthians 13:7 is basic to the
improvement of any relationship and helps a couple sense what
a truly open and positive love relationship represents—support,
trust, hope and endurance. And it's not only a passage that will
generate hope for the hurting spouse, but it is also one that we
as counselors need if we have concern about a person's ability to
change.

MEET YOUR NEEDS

As a counselor, many of the couples you see will be engaging in
several predictable negative patterns of behavior—blaming, complaining and withdrawing from their spouses. Discussed in
chapter 6 but expanded here, the behavior-values approach you
can introduce to couples is purposed to help them respond positively and cooperatively to one another. After this is accomplished, they can then form a more promising relationship by
being able to meet each other's needs. It is a fairly simple process
involving five steps:

1. Identify specifically what each spouse would like from
   his or her spouse.
2. Teach both spouses to express this in a positive way,
   rather than focusing on what isn't wanted.

3. Encourage each one to become an explorer, to discover what the mate would like and then surprise that person. They both need to learn to do the unexpected.

4. Encourage each one to thank and compliment his or her spouse each time a positive response is received.

5. Urge each one to pray every day, thanking God for the positive characteristics and responses from his or her spouse, and specifically share with God his or her intentions for his or her own behaviors that day.

By following these steps, the couple has the opportunity to begin to challenge the negative beliefs each has about the other.

This five-step approach accomplishes several objectives. It will change responses from negative to positive, make couples respond specifically rather than vaguely, change the atmosphere from adversarial to cooperative, change their attitude from despair to hopeful and give the couple a positive vision. It also helps each person refocus attention from himself or herself to his or her spouse. And most important, it introduces a biblical basis for resolving problems. According to Ephesians 4:32 and Colossians 3:12-14, each spouse needs to take the responsibility to reach out in love first, rather than to make responses based upon what the spouse does.

The following dialogue tells a story about Jim and Janice, who seek help from their pastor in order to figure out why they feel like they don't get along anymore. They wonder if staying together is worth the effort. They've been attending church for five years but have never really become involved. Janice says she is resentful that Jim pays so little attention to her and is seldom home to assist her. Jim is upset over the constant pressure to talk to her and help her. He's tired of being criticized. Read on to discover the outcome.

Pastor: Janice, what three things could Jim do to make you feel better? To actually please you?

Janice: He could be home more, keep the TV off and help me. It's not easy you know with—

Pastor (Interrupting.): Could you share specifically what you would like him to do?

Janice: I would like it if he cleaned the yard, helped with the children and let me know if he's going to be late for dinner.

Pastor: Janice, when Jim does these things this next week, how will it make you feel?

Janice: I think I would feel better about him and more hopeful about our marriage.

Pastor: When you say "help with the children," what do you mean? Can you be more specific? And share this with Jim directly now, would you?

Janice: Well, you never seem to know that I need help with—

Pastor (Interrupting.): Could you say what it is you would like him to do, rather than talking about what he doesn't do?

Janice: I would like you to start asking me how you could help, and at least twice a week bathe the children and put them to bed.

Pastor: Jim, what is it that Janice could do for you?

Jim: Quit nagging and criticizing me, give me some space to recover from work and quit pressuring me about our financial condition.

Pastor: I'm not sure I understand what you mean by nagging.

Jim: Well, I'll tell you. She goes on and on about what she doesn't like, including my work hours, not making enough money, not understanding the kids, how

I dress. Is that enough? It is for me. I don't like being criticized so much.

Pastor: So you've said that what you want Janice to do to please you is to quit criticizing and nagging you, give you some time alone and get off your case about money. Now will you please tell her what you would like her to do, rather than what you don't want? Would you turn to her and share this?

Jim: I want you to let me know what I do right. I'm gone a lot trying to make more money, and sometimes I'm exhausted at night. Let me recover for a half hour and I'll be fit to live with. And when I do dress the way you like, tell me about that, rather than when you think I'm a slob.

Pastor: Janice, do you now understand what Jim wants from you?

Janice: I think so. Some trial and error may be involved, but I think I can figure it out.

Pastor: What about you, Jim? Do you see what it is that Janice needs from you?

Jim: Yes, it's pretty clear to me.

Pastor: What exactly will you be doing this week? Would you turn and share with Janice what you will do this week?

Jim: I think so, but I want her to make some changes, too.

Pastor: Jim, it will be better if you just take the initiative to make some changes independent of what Janice does.

Jim: I can do that. Janice, I will ask you every other day if I can do something to help. I'll work in the yard one, no, two hours this week when I can work it in. And

let's see, okay, on Tuesday and Friday nights I'll take
care of the "bath and bed" struggle with the kids.

The session continued with Janice stating what she would do,
and then each was asked to write out their intentions, sign it and
leave it with their pastor. The pastor concluded the session by
praying for them and stating that he would pray for them each
day and suggested they think about how they could pray for one
another.

This is just one of many behavioral approaches that once
implemented can help couples meet each other's needs. The
approach is structured and didactic in nature and teaches couples relationship skills in an open and direct format. As a result,
the counseling couple will be able to generalize the principles
they've learned concerning a specific conflict area and apply
those principles to other areas of their life.

Chapter 8

OVERCOME CONFLICT

Session Five

It is important to deal with conflict and anger toward the end of the six sessions. As a counselor, you ideally want to focus on the positives in the first few sessions in order to increase confidence and to avoid instilling an early feeling of defeat in the counselees. Yet conflict is a normal part of marriage, and it eventually needs to be exposed and dealt with. Unfortunately, many couples have not been taught how to handle conflict in a positive, healthy manner. The word "conflict" actually means "to strike together." Webster defines it as a "clash, competition, or mutual interference of opposing or incompatible forces or qualities (as ideas, interests, wills)."[1]

Many marriages you counsel are characterized by strife and bickering, rather than peace and harmony. It is never safe to assume that couples who have developed harmony are identical in their thinking, behavior and attitudes. This is dangerous to assume because people are not carbon copies of each other.

Couples with a peaceful relationship have learned to accept their differences through the processes of acceptance, understanding and eventually complementation. They have learned to deal with

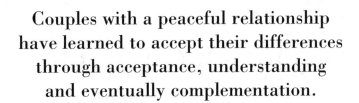

Couples with a peaceful relationship have learned to accept their differences through acceptance, understanding and eventually complementation.

their conflicts in a positive way, so they need to focus on the positives early on in counseling. Differing from another person is natural and normal and adds an edge of excitement to a relationship.

As one therapist reflected upon conflict:

> If there is one lesson I have learned from my years of research it is that *a lasting marriage results from a couple's ability to resolve the conflicts that are inevitable in any relationship.* Many couples tend to equate a low level of conflict with happiness and believe the claim "we never fight" is a sign of marital health. But I believe we grow in our relationships by reconciling our differences. That's how we become more loving people and truly experience the fruits of marriage.
>
> But there's much more to know than how to fight well. Not all stable couples resolve conflicts in the same way. Nor do all couples mean the same thing by "resolving" conflict. In fact, I have found that there are three

different styles of problem solving into which healthy marriages tend to settle. In a *validating marriage* couples compromise often and calmly work out their problems to mutual satisfaction as they arise. In a *conflict-avoiding marriage* couples agree to disagree, rarely confronting their differences head-on. And finally, in a *volatile marriage* conflicts erupt often, resulting in passionate disputes.[2]

By just accepting the fact that each person is unique and what each person brings to the marriage is unique, conflict is inevitable. In fact, many conflicts will occur throughout the life of the marriage.

Additionally, for many couples the normal day-to-day conflicts are not resolved, so they escalate into ongoing feuds. Over the years I've heard many couples say, "It isn't that we haven't talked about the problem. We've talked and fought about it for 15 years. We just don't know how to resolve it!" The intensity of anger and frustration within the marital relationship varies greatly. For some, individual therapy may be necessary to overcome the lifelong accumulation of hurt and inappropriate patterns of response.

Also keep in mind the effect gender differences have in conflict. Usually, men have a harder time handling conflict with their wives, so they tend to withdraw, while women have a harder time with emotional distance and tend to want to discuss and settle each problem, rather than put it off.

The author of *Why Marriages Succeed or Fail* describes gender differences in this way:

Wives are often the caretakers of intimacy in marriages, so they wind up being the ones to bring up issues. Women have better memories for social events than men, and are better at not getting so upset and disorganized by strong negative emotions. Men are more likely to want to avoid conflict when the negative emotions get intense. They try to be rational, conciliatory, and tend to rush too quickly toward a rational attempt to "solve" the problem (usually meaning to make it go away) before really understanding and empathizing with their wife's feelings.[3]

Do you see how gender differences potentially cause conflict if not recognized as a source and then dealt with constructively in a marriage?

FIVE CONFLICT STYLES

Over the years, I've noticed that when couples begin sharing their difficulties, they will use words and phrases that are subjective and need defining. For example, "We fight constantly"; "We have so many conflicts" and "He abuses me and the children" need clarification. What does someone mean by "constantly"—every minute they are together? What is a conflict? What kind of abuse? Since every individual perceives and means words differently, it is very important to clarify.

Often as you begin working with couples who experience typical marital conflicts, it is helpful first to identify their fight, or conflictual, pattern. We do this by actually showing a visualized presentation of these patterns. The following diagram is shared with the couple on a flip chart or chalkboard (or whatever you feel comfortable in using) as you describe the various styles. Your description for each style should not contain any biased language, because couples will pick up on the value judgments and perhaps use them against each other after the session.

Five Conflict Styles

Yield   **Resolve**

Compromise

Withdraw   **Win**

The counselor begins by explaining that most people use one of five basic styles, or methods, of dealing with marital conflict.

Withdrawal

People who tend to see conflict as inevitable and who think they can do little to control it may not even bother to try. They may withdraw physically by removing themselves from the room or from the environment. Other times they may withdraw psychologically by ignoring the other person, by refusing to speak or by insulating themselves so carefully that what is said or suggested has no penetrating power.

Win

If people's self-concepts are threatened or if they feel strongly that they must look after their own interests, then winning may be their choice. Winning is a way of counterattacking when a person's position of authority is threatened.

People employ a variety of tactics in order to win. Because married couples are well aware of each other's areas of vulnerability and hurt, they often use these areas to coerce the other person into giving in to their demands. "Winners" may attack self-esteem or pride to win. They may store up grudges and use them at the appropriate time to take care of a conflict. They may cash in on old emotions and hurts at an opportune moment. Winning becomes the goal regardless of the cost, and although the goal may be achieved, it is sometimes at the expense of the relationship.

Yield

We often see yield signs on the highway; they are placed there for our own protection. When people yield in conflict, they are protecting themselves. They do not want to risk a confrontation, so they give in to get along with their spouses.

We all use this approach from time to time, but yielding sometimes becomes a regular pattern. Consistent yielding may create feelings of martyrdom or eventually guilt.

Compromise

A spouse who backs off some of his or her ideas or demands helps his or her spouse give a little. This approach involves concessions on both sides and has been called the horse-trading technique. Yet such concessions can leave one or both spouses dissatisfied with the results. Sometimes the bargaining involved means some values are compromised. Couples may have a feeling of uneasiness following the settlement, even though one or both spouses think, *Well, it's better than nothing.* Such a situation could actually threaten the relationship.

Resolve

In this style of dealing with conflicts, a situation, attitude or behavior is changed by open and direct communication. The couple is willing to spend sufficient time working on the difference so that although some of their original wants and ideas have changed, they are satisfied with their solution. Resolve is the most desirable method.

FOUR CONFLICT STRATEGIES

Another way of looking at conflict is to consider the strategy each spouse selects and then the resulting kind of conflict interaction. Again, it would be helpful to prepare a chart for your counselees, so they can identify their respective styles and the resulting interactions.

Despite the positive intent we know spouses have when confronting relationship conflict, once conflict gets going it will leave spouses feeling aroused and perhaps overwhelmed. When our emotions run high and our communication and conflict-resolution skills are low, we tend to handle threats to security and well-being by duking it out or running away. Couples will always have two strategies that guide the response to conflict—his and hers.

If we consider the possible pairing of his and her strategies, we can summarize the four types of relationship conflict as follows:

Her Strategy	+	His Strategy	=	Relationship Conflict Type
Fight	+	Fight	=	Escalation
Flee	+	Flee	=	Withdrawal
Fight	+	Flee	=	Pursuit + Withdrawal
Flee	+	Fight	=	Withdrawal + Pursuit

When any one of these four conflict types becomes the standard way of reacting to disagreements, relationships will suffer over the long run. The pursuit + withdrawal pattern is twice as harmful because couples function very differently depending on who acts which role. In my experience, it is far more common to see female pursuers and male withdrawers than it is to see these positions reversed. And as long as one spouse adopts one of these destructive strategies, the relationship will be at risk.

Every couple from time to time will find themselves embroiled in an escalating fight, chilled by the emotional coolness created by mutual withdrawal or frustrated by the relationship tug-of-war that results when one spouse pushes for peace through talk and the other pushes for peace through avoidance of conflict.[4] However, the important thing is not to let your "preferred" strategies turn into habit.

After the couple has identified their conflict or fight strategy, the counselor can present alternatives for resolving conflict. Many guidelines for handling disagreements are available for you to share with couples. Two important guidelines you can share with the couple are to recognize conflict issues and to listen carefully to the other person.

Recognize Conflict Issues

To be aware of issues that cause conflict is not to be looking for a fight. But when disagreements do arise, each spouse can accept them as opportunities to develop understanding of one another. Consequently, the period of resolving conflict can be a time of growth. The attitude of the couple—whether pessimistic or optimistic—will influence and determine the outcome!

Listen Carefully to the Other Person

Proverbs 18:13 says it is "folly" and "shame" to one who gives an answer before he hears, and James 1:19 in *The Living Bible* reminds us that "it is best to listen much, speak little, and not become angry." Whenever couples listen to each other, they discover that their spouses begin to take them seriously and even start to listen. It is vital that each spouse hears and understands any changes their spouse desires.

Here is how one marriage counselor describes the problems of listening and how he helps couples in counseling learn to listen better:

> Most people are really very poor listeners. They "hear" with preconceived prejudices; they generally twist and misinterpret much that is said to them and often only hear what they want to. It seems to me, therefore, that an essential part of therapy—particularly when one is working with two people, as in a marriage, a parent-child relationship or some form of partnership—is to aid individuals to say clearly what they mean and to learn to listen openly in order to hear accurately what the other person is attempting to say.
>
> I ask couples seen in joint therapy sessions to use the "feedback" technique repeatedly to facilitate understanding each other and to get their message across. "We're going to try an experiment," I told the Rogers. "Obviously, the two of you aren't going anywhere the way you're going at talking, and I have found a method that really proves helpful to people. I imagine that most of the talking at home between the two of you is just like what you were doing right here a minute ago, right?"
>
> Both people nodded vigorously, "Oh, yes." Mary said. "Why, even last night—" her eyes started to fill with tears, and I could tell we were in for another angry tirade.

"Hold it," I said firmly. "Continuing to blame each other for faults and shortcomings is, as we've discussed before, the opposite of rationally accepting the things other people say and do, even when what they do is admittedly poor. We don't have to like what people do, but we do have to accept what they do and say because that's reality. Then we can go ahead and try to change some of the ways that other people act, to see if we can get the world to be more the way we'd like it. But the way the two of you are trying to change each other doesn't seem to me to be bringing you the kinds of results that you both have repeatedly told me you want. So let's try something new, okay?"

I went on then to outline the ground rules for the "feedback" technique. First, one spouse could say anything he or she wanted—bring up a problem, "bitch" about something, etc. I instructed them to try to keep it fairly brief. During the time one person was talking the other was not allowed to interrupt or say anything. When the first person had had his or her say, then the other person was to say back to the first person the gist of what had been communicated. He or she did not have to use exactly the same words or terms, but what was important was to try to say back the *meaning* of what the first person had said. The original speaker was then either to agree (yes, that was what he or she had been trying to say) or disagree (no, that was not quite what he or she really meant, or even that it was definitely not the correct interpretation). If the second person did not "feedback" what had been said to the satisfaction of the first person, then the first party was instructed to repeat his or her message.[5]

One variation of the feedback technique as a method of developing listening skills is the use of a communication game. It is called the revolving discussion sequence or RDS.

THE COMMUNICATION GAME

RDS is a noncompetitive game designed to help the couple arrive at a compromise in which no one wins at the expense of the other.

The game is played with simple rules. First, one spouse makes a statement. Before the other spouse can reply, he or she must restate, to the first person's satisfaction, what was said. When a clear understanding has been established from what the first person said to what the second person heard, the second person must find a way to agree with it. If there is total agreement, then there is no problem. However, if the second person does not agree entirely with what the first person said, the second person can reply in a manner such as, "I can agree there's considerable truth in what you say." Or the second person may grudgingly admit, "There's a grain of truth there." However, if the second person does not agree at all, he or she simply agrees that this is how his or her spouse thinks and affirms his or her right to that opinion.

After the statement, restatement and agreement, the second person is free to make his or her statement. Again, before the first person can reply, he or she must restate, to the satisfaction of the second person, what that person said and find a way to agree with it. This process is continued until the matter is resolved. The rules are simple: state, restate and agree; state, restate and agree.[6] By emphasizing listening and understanding, the counselor helps the couple learn to replace insults and accusations with positive statements.

EFFECTIVE COMMUNICATION STRATEGIES

Sometimes effective communication merely means listening attentively to each other. There are two important concepts I feel help couples listen and share without conflict.

Select the Most Appropriate Time

Scripture says, "How wonderful it is to be able to say the right thing at the right time!" (Prov. 15:23, *TLB*). If one or both spouses are hungry, fatigued or emotionally upset, or if time is limited, perhaps because of an appointment or work schedule, encourage spouses to delay problem solving. Couples should agree to a definite time, rather than saying "later." This is because "later" has a different meaning for each person.

The time selected should allow for the greatest understanding and cooperative effort. Both parties should know what the subject or issue is beforehand and know when it will be discussed. In this way, each person can practice what he or she wants to say and how to say it. The individuals then also have the opportunity to think about his or her feelings and needs.

Make It Easy for Your Spouse to Respond

In a conflict it helps for both spouses to share what they want by making statements of preference, not necessity. If one spouse feels unloved by his or her spouse, one way to communicate that need is to initiate loving behavior toward the spouse.

Often when we think others do not love us, we may believe we are not worth loving. If you begin to perform loving acts, your spouse might act more loving toward you, but if not, that's alright. Your act of love can fulfill some of your own needs and is also a demonstration of Christ's love toward others. Remember that real marital love is an unconditional commitment to an imperfect person.

MORE EFFECTIVE COMMUNICATION STRATEGIES

Another way to communicate so that couples can respond more easily is to make "I" statements rather than "you" statements, and to share present feelings rather than past thoughts or feelings.

The Minnesota Couples Communication Program started in 1968 and has had more than 600,000 couples participate in its training programs. During these training programs, the authors of the program provide suggested skills for expressing self-awareness. (This is just a small sampling of the program's practical guidelines.) The four suggestions are illustrated so couples can understand each one.

Speaking for Self

The following example shows a couple effectively communicating because they both speak for themselves:

> *Husband:* I'd like to go out tonight.
> *Wife:* I would too. I'd like to eat out at a nice restaurant. How about you?
> *Husband:* I think that's a good idea. I'd like to go to . . .

On the other hand, the underresponsible couple doesn't speak for themselves and doesn't let others know what they want or feel (or tries not to anyway). They usually say things in an indirect way, often making sweeping generalizations about what "everyone" thinks or feels, like the following examples:

1. "Some wives would be angry at your staying out all night."
2. "Other guys expect their wives to look good when they go out together."

The following interchange describes people who try to avoid being candid about their own thoughts, feelings and intentions. Often they are put in the position of denying their own thoughts, feelings and intentions, almost as if they were a nobody.

> *Wife:* Some wives would be angry at your staying out all night.
> *Husband:* You mad or something?
> *Wife:* Oh, no, I'm not. But some wives would be.

Another type of person—the overresponsible—leaves out the "I." This person's problem is trying to speak for the other person instead of for himself or herself. So he or she says what the other person thinks or feels or intends. To do this, he or she usually sends "you messages."

1. "You don't like that kind of TV program."
2. "You're pretty tired tonight, aren't you?"
3. "You want to go on a fishing trip this year, don't you?"

When you presume to speak for someone else, you proclaim that you are an expert on what the other person thinks, feels or intends. You tell him or her that you know what is going on in his or her mind—maybe even better than he or she does. But can you really?

A close variation of speaking for yourself is what is called the

"I message." It is very helpful in resolving conflicts. "I messages" are messages that identify where the speaker is and thus are more oriented to the speaker than to the listener. The speaker may want to modify the behavior of another person, change a situation or simply identify his or her position or feeling. An "I message" is distinguished from a "you message" in that the speaker claims the problem as his or her own. For example, instead of saying "You make me so mad," an "I message" would say "I feel very angry when you do that."

An "I message" consists of three parts: the feeling, the situation and how the message affects the sender. It is a statement of fact, rather than an evaluation, and, therefore, is less likely to lower the other person's self-esteem. It is also less likely to provoke resistance, anger or resentment and is, therefore, less likely to hurt the relationship. The "I message" is risky because it may reveal the humanness of the speaker, and the listener may use this vulnerability against the speaker. But it helps a person connect closer to his or her own feelings and needs. It models honesty and openness.

Documenting

Documenting is making statements with descriptive behavioral data.

> *Husband:* I think you're elated. I see a smile on your face, and your voice sounds lyrical to me.

Documenting is an important skill. First, it increases your own understanding of yourself. It gives you a better idea of how you arrived at your own thoughts, feelings and intentions. At the same time, it gives the other person a much clearer idea of what you are responding to.

Making Feeling Statements

When you make a feeling statement, you don't know how the other person will respond. Therefore, feeling statements are risky.

> *Wife:* I feel sick to my stomach when I see you bow and scrape to your boss.

Do you see how the wife openly expressed her feelings toward her husband's actions toward his boss? There are four main ways to describe feelings verbally:

1. Identify or name the feeling: "I feel angry." "I feel sad." "I feel good about you."
2. Use similes or metaphors; we do not always have enough labels to describe our emotions, so we sometimes invent similes and metaphors to describe feelings: "I felt squelched." "I felt like a cool breeze going through the air."
3. Report the type of action your feelings urge you to do: "I feel like hugging you." "I wish I could hit you."
4. Use figures of speech: "The sun is smiling on me today." "I feel like a dark cloud is following me around today."

Making Intention Statements

Intention statements are ways of expressing your immediate goals or desires in a situation. These statements provide information about you to the other person—an overview of what you are willing to do.

> *Wife:* I want very much to end this argument.
> *Husband:* I didn't know that. I thought you were too mad to stop.

These four communication strategies help couples express self-awareness—an important step to take. Why? Because spouses who are aware of their own behaviors, thoughts and communication styles—before they begin pointing out their spouse's shortfalls in these areas—will move to conflict resolution quicker.[7]

STEPS TO OVERCOME CONFLICT

Often couples experience conflict over how one spouse handles the other's feelings. Denial of a person's feelings is commonly expressed with statements such as "You shouldn't feel that way" or "That's all in your head. Don't let it bother you." Whether to have or not have feelings cannot be legislated. And what is unimportant to one spouse may be very important to another. When a wife tells her husband he shouldn't feel a certain way, you might

It often helps to have the couple put their feelings into writing.

suggest, "You know, feelings are hard to legislate for another person. Could we accept the fact that your husband has those feelings and talk about what he could do that you would prefer more?" This is just one suggested tactic. However, the following five guidelines will provide you a step-by-step approach on how to counsel couples through conflict effectively. It is based on my book *Communication and Conflict Resolution in Marriage*.

1. Define the Conflict Problem Specifically
It often helps to have the couple put their feelings into writing

because, although it is time-consuming, writing helps them understand how a problem relates to unfulfilled needs. It helps the couple see the relationship based on their own views of the conflict and the basic psychological need that may have authored it. In defining the issue, each spouse must consider both his or her own behavior, his or her spouse's behavior, as well as the environment.

It is often beneficial to have each person ask the following questions of himself or herself when trying to clarify the problem: How do I define the problem? How do I think the other person defines the problem? In my opinion, what behaviors contribute to the conflict? What behaviors do I think the other person sees as contributing to the conflict? What are the issues of agreement and disagreement in this conflict?

The more narrowly the conflict is defined, the easier conflict resolution will be. Often it helps if each person will write out a response to each question. When the person sees the answer, it affects him or her in a more significant way.

As couples fight or disagree, they tend to lump together feelings, intentions and behaviors. It is common to find that when a negative feeling is provoked in a person, he or she blames the other for purposely using the behavior that created the response. "You come home late on purpose just to make me angry." "You didn't go to the store like I asked just to get back at me." Feelings distort one person's evaluation of another person's behavior. If this occurs, the focus needs to turn to the person's assumptions and beliefs concerning behavior and help him or her learn how to challenge his or her own beliefs.

2. Identify Your Own Contribution to the Problem

In trying to resolve conflicts, the couple is basically saying to each other, "We have a problem." The way they approach one another and the words they use will be important in this step. When one person accepts some responsibility for a problem, the other senses a spirit of cooperation. Often this helps the couple to be more open in the discussion. Here is an approach to use to open a discussion:

Choose one word that best indicates what you want to talk about. State the word or the subject that you want to talk about in one complete sentence. Be precise and specific. Try not to blame, ridicule or attack your partner, and do not overload him or her with too much information all at once.

Take responsibility for the problem, and tell your partner the reason that you are bringing this matter up for discussion. For example, "I have a problem. I have something that is a little difficult for me to talk about, but our relationship is very important to me, and by talking about it I feel that we will have a better relationship. I feel that _____ is the problem, and this is what I am contributing to it . . . I would like to hear what you think and how you feel about it." Any statement similar to this is a very healthy way of expressing yourself and approaching what otherwise might be an explosive confrontation.

If your partner approaches you in this manner, respond by saying, "Thank you for telling me. If I understand what you feel, the problem is _____. I can agree that you feel this way." Restate the problem to make sure you have correctly understood your partner.

The conflict may be the result of a specific behavior of the other person. Take for example a husband who does not pick up after himself. His wife approaches him with a typical response: "Time after time I've asked you to pick up your things. Good grief! You couldn't be this sloppy at work or you wouldn't keep your job. I'm sick of this. I'm not picking up one more item around here after you. What kind of example are you to the children?"

Contrast that to the wife who selects a proper time and approaches her husband by saying, "Dear, I have a problem and I feel that I need to talk to you about it. Perhaps I have not shared my real feelings with you, but I am bothered by our differences in neatness around the house. I would feel better toward you and less resentful if I felt you were helping by picking up your clothes in the morning and putting your work away from the night before. If this were done I would feel better and actually have more time. How do you feel about it?"[8]

Of course, the statements above are only examples. The couple must choose their own words. They should be encouraged to be explicit when sharing not only their spouse's undesirable behaviors but also their own behaviors that the spouse probably finds unacceptable.

3. Identify Alternatives

After the couple has identified their individual contributions to the problem, the next step is to find a solution that would be advantageous to both. Each person should think of as many solutions as possible and consider behavior changes in both spouses. Posing a number of alternatives promotes flexibility and eliminates an "either-or" solution. All proposed alternatives should meet the needs of each spouse.

4. Decide on a Mutually Acceptable Solution

The couple should then identify and evaluate each possible solution. In evaluating, they should consider the steps in bringing the solution about and the possible outcome of each alternative. They should ask themselves what each person will have to change if a given alternative is chosen, and how the change will affect the marriage and the behaviors of each spouse.

Sometimes one spouse will like an alternative the other finds unacceptable. In such a situation, they should discuss the reasons for their preference. Sharing in this way can prevent feelings of rejection.

5. Implement New Behaviors

Couples should be encouraged to concentrate individually on their own behavior changes, not on the changes the spouse is making. After the changes have occurred, the couple should evaluate their effects upon the relationship.[9]

Many models of resolving conflict can be taught to couples, whether it be in classes or premarital or marital counseling. The authors of *We Can Work it Out* suggest that a couple meet together and discuss and answer four questions:

1. What is the problem?
2. What are possible solutions to the problem?
3. What solutions will we try?
4. How will we evaluate our successes?[10]

Additionally, the authors discuss how these questions effect the couple as they move through the following six stages of problem-solving:

1. Relating—understanding and validating each other
2. Focusing—narrowing a specific problem to solve
3. Brainstorming—creatively generating potential solutions
4. Selecting—choosing one or two solutions to try out
5. Formalizing—committing to carry out agreement
6. Recycling—integrating successful solutions into your relationship[11]

Resolving conflict does not have to be difficult. Plus, didn't you notice how most resolution comes from the idea of focusing on the positive, which is similar to what we've discussed throughout the preceding four sessions? Carry on with these suggested methods, and you will find that couples can and will resolve conflict easier.

Chapter 9

GIVE UP ANGER

Session Six

Resolving anger is the final area highlighted within the six-sessions-or-less counseling style. Because many couples struggle with anger, it is important to know how to help your counselees through this potentially destructive emotion. How can you help counselees resolve anger? The following dialogue depicts what can happen when a counselor directs a couple to resolve anger by incorporating many of the concepts we've learned so far: focusing on the positive, noticing the exceptions and applying the change-first principle. You may want to take notes of what this minister did during the session.

> *Minister:* I'm interested in hearing about your week, especially the times when you were problem solving.
>
> *Dan:* We did a lot of talking, but I'm not too sure I saw any problems solved. It was more like a rehash of what went on before.
>
> *Minister:* So from your perspective, you talked about issues

you previously discussed. What was different about it
this time?

Dan: I guess the only thing that was different was it
didn't go on forever and, well, I wasn't as angry.

Minister: So you're saying it might have been better in a
small way?

Dan: Yeah, very small. But I guess any progress is better
than none at all.

Minister: That's true. Before you came today, were you conscious that it was a step in the right direction?

Dan (Pauses.): I guess not. You're probably suggesting that
I ought to keep my eyes open and notice the small
steps of progress, right?

Minister: I can see you've been listening. That's progress. I
have a question for you. When I ask Jean how she felt
about this past week, what might she say was better
for her?

Dan: I'm not really sure.

Minister: What would you hope she would say?

Dan: I think I would like her to say—

Minister (Interrupting.): Would you turn to Jean and talk to
her directly?

Dan: Jean, I, uh, I think I would hope to hear you say, if not
today, then sometime in the future, that during the
past week I listened to you a little better and didn't
interrupt you as much. I, if I don't get as angry, hope
that you would notice any improvement no matter
how small it is and let me know about it. I need to hear
from you that you notice my efforts and that it means
something to you. It's hard to make changes anyway
and worse when they go unrecognized. I'm trying to
stay in the discussions with you, and the half-hour

time limit gives me some hope that we won't be talking all night, but pressuring me to talk doesn't work—

Minister: You changed directions.

Dan: What do you mean?

Minister: You changed from sharing what you thought or hoped she would say to lecturing and blaming, and your tone of voice started to become intense. This is a pattern that's happened for years, isn't it?

Dan: I don't think I did that.

Minister: Let me back up the tape recorder and listen to what you shared. (The pastor rewinds the tape, so Dan can hear what he said and how he said it.) Dan, what's your response to what you heard?

Dan (Pauses.): Tape recorders don't lie, do they? I guess I did shift into blaming, and my tone became more definite, more intense, more—

Minister: More angry?

Dan: Yes, more angry

Minister: In the future as you become more aware of your tendency, what will you do when you catch yourself blaming or becoming angry?

Dan: I think I will—

Minister: Would you turn and tell Jean directly?

Dan: This is different. . . . Jean, what I want to say to you is, uh, I want to be different, but it's not that easy. In the future if or when I start to blame or get angry, and if I recognize it, I will say, "That's not what I wanted to say, and this is what I want to say." Yeah, I like that. I think I could do that if I'm aware that I'm being a jerk again.

Minister: I hear you're wanting to be aware, but you're not too sure you can recognize it. Do you need Jean to give you some assistance?

Dan: That might be helpful, even though I'd rather be able to do it myself, but I don't have the confidence that I can.

Minister: What could Jean say in the meantime to help you until you develop the ability to interrupt your old negative patterns? What can she say or do that you won't take offense to and become even more upset?

Dan: Hmmm. That's a good point. I guess you're saying I have to give her permission to say something along with the reassurance I'm not going to get ticked off at her for doing it. Right?

Minister: You're right. It's up to you to decide, give her some guidance and then don't bite her head off when she does.

Dan: That will be new. Okay, here goes. Jean, when you hear me blaming you or getting angry, maybe you could say either "blame" or "anger" and that would help me recognize what I'm doing so I can correct it.

Minister: That's an excellent suggestion. And what can she expect from you in terms of assurance when she does this?

Dan: I think she can—

Minister (Interrupting.): Tell Jean.

Dan: I will accept what you say. I might stop talking for a while to regroup and get my emotions under control, and then I'll respond. Don't assume that I'm going to withdraw, because I won't. I agree to that.

Minister: Jean, we've dominated the time so far talking with Dan and talking with you some of the time. Before you and I talk, is it alright for me to ask him one more question about you?

Jean: Yes, certainly. And I guess I'm curious about what it is.

Minister: Dan, how do think Jean might be feeling right now after this interchange? Not what she thinks, but how she feels.

Dan: You're still after me to get into that feeling stuff, aren't you?

Minister: Yes, especially if you want to speak her language and for the two of you to be on the same level.

Dan: I guess Jean may be feeling that, uh, there may be some hope for our relationship. Hopeful, yeah, that might be the word. I don't think she's joyful or elated, but maybe encouraged. How are those words?

Minister: Excellent. You're able to do it. You're open to learning. The next step is sharing how you feel, but we'll deal with that later. Jean, how do you feel about what you've heard so far?

Jean: I had mixed feelings about the past week, but I wasn't as negative about it as Dan. The fact that he didn't withdraw, even when my mouth started working overtime again, was encouraging. And then to hear for the first time a definite plan and a commitment to doing something different does encourage me. Honestly I do wonder what will happen when I say the words "blame" or "anger." I hope it works. I want it to work. But I am apprehensive.

Minister: What will you do if there is a negative response to your calling Dan back to his commitment? Will you tell him right now?

Jean: Dan, first of all, I believe that you want to be different and speak differently. You can do it. If there's a relapse, I will just repeat what I said before. No, I'll do more than that. I'll write them on cards and hold them up, so you can read them. Our pastor has said you respond best to seeing things, so I'll do that. And when you do anything positive, I'll notice and let you know. I need the same from you.

Minister: So you're willing to respond in a positive way, even if there is a relapse? Both of you seem to have the desire to make your relationship different. And you both want your efforts to be recognized by the other.

While this dialogue provides one approach on how to handle abusive and angry spouses, many other approaches are available. In this chapter several suggestions will be given to you to use with couples in counseling.

ELIMINATING ANGER

Here is a practical seven-step program for resolving anger. It can be diagrammed on a flip chart and explained in detail to a couple or an individual.

1. Identify the Cues That Contribute to the Anger

The first step is to assess the couple's communication pattern in order to discover how and when they express anger toward one another. You need to look for what brings about the anger and what keeps it going. The purpose is to discover the causes and not to lay blame on either spouse. Each spouse must learn to recognize the early signs of anger, especially his or her tendencies, and then change his or her responses toward one another.

2. Establish "Fair Fight" Rules

"Fair fight" rules should not include personal attacks or references to a spouse's tone of voice, facial expressions, style of communication, etc. Rather, the rules should reflect a couple's compromise on how to deal with conflict. For example, if a husband wants to walk away to think about an issue and then discuss it, while the wife wants to discuss it immediately, a compromise on how to deal with that particular scenario needs to be agreed upon by both spouses.

3. Develop a Plan of Action for Interrupting the Conflict Pattern

This plan should involve immediate action that disengages the couple from conflict and also gives the couple a way to face and handle the problem at a later time. Interrupting the conflict is an application of Nehemiah 5:6-7 (*AMP*): "I [Nehemiah] was very angry when I heard their cry and these words. I thought it over and then rebuked the nobles and officials."

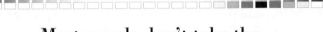

Most people don't take the time to admit, scrutinize and then handle their anger.

The neutral expressions "I'm getting angry," "I'm losing control," "We're starting to fight" and "I'm going to write out my feelings" are also positive steps. Upon hearing such a statement, the listening spouse could share a developed phrase such as, "Thank you for telling me. What is it that I could do that would help right now?"

A commitment from both spouses not to yell or raise their voices and not to act out their anger is essential. This step is called suspending the anger. It is a positive move when couples agree to return to the issue at a less conflictual time. Most people don't take the time to admit, scrutinize and then handle their anger. These steps and procedures should be practiced and rehearsed through role-play in your presence.

The interruption period can be an opportune time for the spouses to focus upon their own anger. In counseling, it is important to teach counselees how to discover the cause of their anger, so in the future they will be able to respond with less anger.

Anger stems from three basic causes. One cause is *hurt*. When a person experiences hurt (such as rejection, criticism or physical or emotional pain), the normal response is anger. Another cause is *fear*. A person who senses he or she is in a vulnerable position and doesn't like feeling vulnerable will counter with anger. A third cause is *frustration*. Frustration occurs in many forms. Usually it is an indication that a person's needs and/or expectations are being blocked. There will be an elevation of anger in a person who wants something and feels thwarted. In order to forestall the three causes of anger, it's important to take action by following these three steps from Aaron Beck's book *Love Is Never Enough*:

1. When you feel strong anger toward your spouse, sit down and write down your feelings. Write honestly, passionately—just as you feel. Exclamation points and underlining is allowed. Also write down the reason for your anger. Identify the cause. If you prefer, write an angry letter to your mate. Again, be honest about your feelings. You may read the letter out loud in an empty room. Then destroy the letter.

2. Once you have reviewed the list of what you wrote (or destroyed the letter), set up a meeting time for an

anger ventilation session with your spouse. Then discuss the causes of your anger.

3. After your spouse and you hold an anger ventilation session, complete the following anger expression form. This form can be used when identifying the positive and negative effects of your anger toward your spouse. (The form is also helpful when dealing with anger in other relationships outside the marriage.) This will be your own perception and, thus, could be different from your spouse's perception.[1]

Have your counselees fill out the following anger expression form. It is best to create a numbered list of the positive and negative results and have each spouse place a checkmark by the statements he or she believes are true.

Positive Results

1. My spouse responded better after I expressed my anger.
2. I felt better after expressing my anger.
3. I feel my spouse felt better after the interchange. (It would be helpful if you asked him or her about this.)
4. Becoming angry protected me when my spouse became upset.
5. My spouse gained a clearer understanding of my position because of my anger.
6. I feel closer to my spouse because of expressing my anger.
7. Becoming angry helped solve the problem, so we won't need to experience it again.
8. We felt more loving toward one another because of expressing anger.
9. My expression of anger involved a more constructive

statement than provocative.

10. We learned from this experience so that our next disagreement should be better.

Negative Results

1. In expressing my anger, I was so upset that I didn't clarify my position well.
2. I made statements or behaved in a way that I now regret.
3. My spouse did not accept what I said.
4. My spouse had difficulty hearing me because of my anger.
5. My spouse became upset because of my anger and became very emotional.
6. My spouse was hurt by my anger.
7. My spouse is still recovering from my anger.
8. My anger prolonged the disagreement and hindered us from finding a solution.
9. Our next disagreement will probably be more difficult because of my anger.
10. We really didn't learn from this experience.[2]

Another way to interrupt anger and help a person identify the causes of his or her anger is to introduce him or her to the concept of a "Stop! Think!" card. On one side of a 3x5-inch card, the word "Stop!" is written. The other side contains the following three questions: Am I experiencing hurt over something right now? Am I in some way afraid? Am I frustrated over a need or expectation? The minute the person begins to experience anger, he or she is to take out the card, read the word "Stop!" twice (out loud if possible) and then turn the card over and read and respond to the three questions. Another advantage to the card is that reading it is a beneficial delaying tactic to control the anger.

4. Eliminate Trigger Behaviors

We are not responsible for another person's anger, and spousal abuse is never acceptable. However, if one spouse has certain behaviors that tend to provoke, or trigger, anger from the other spouse, these behaviors could be eliminated, so the first spouse doesn't have any reason to retaliate. Minor or defensive behaviors can be a trigger. Leaving clothes on the floor or a hair dryer on the sink in the bathroom, referring to the past, and banging pots and pans are triggers that are easy to change. If a spouse's cowering elicits abusiveness, he or she can leave the room before the abuse occurs. In determining the cues, it may be important for couples to talk through some of their episodes in order to discover specific triggers and then seek alternatives.

5. Change Faulty Thinking Patterns

Here again, the problem of expectations and assumptions arises. The faulty beliefs will need to be both exposed and challenged. The following are some common themes:

- "You won't love me if I tell you how I really feel."
- "You won't love me if I disagree with you."
- "It's better just to hide how I feel."
- "It's better to fake it and go along with what he wants."
- "Even if I do speak up, you'll win anyway."
- "She should know what I need."
- "All anger is wrong so I'm not going to express any."
- "I'm not going to lower myself and get angry the way he does."

A biblical approach to anger and disagreement can help a couple develop a more realistic belief system in regard to conflict. You as the counselor should share a balanced biblical perspective and make sure the couple knows anger is normal. Analyzing and challenging assumptions and eliminating mind reading will also be necessary at this time.

Share a balanced biblical perspective and make sure the couple knows anger is normal.

6. Develop Problem-Solving Skills

To alter a couple's previous pattern of anger, they must develop new communication skills and a definite plan for making decisions and solving problems. They will also need to clarify their expectations and come to an understanding of need fulfillment. The specific guidelines to develop new communication skills include:

- Using neutral language without "gunpowder" words.
- Using positive statements rather than vindictive ones.
- Demonstrating positive behaviors toward one another.
- Having a joint discussion of new rules the couple would like for their relationship.[3]

Following these steps will improve the overall tone of any couple's marriage.

7. Redirect the Focus

Redirect the focus from trying to decide who is right or wrong to determining the behaviors involved and how they affect the relationship.

REDIRECTING ANGER

Listed in the following pages are some additional suggestions that help redirect the focus from anger to more positive interaction.

Prepare a List

A list of written responses to the following questions will assist each spouse in their discussions:

- What angers you about your spouse?
- What is the cause for your anger?
- What do you resent? (One way to identify resentments is to ask them to write "I resent . . . " again and again until they have identified all of the issues.)

Release the Resentment

Overcoming and releasing resentment can be done in a variety of ways. In my counseling, I use an approach that incorporates some of the better techniques currently practiced by many therapists.

These suggestions can also be effective for you. And if a marriage is hindered because of past hurts, these techniques can be effective in releasing resentment whether the person(s) involved is living or deceased.

First, ask the couple to begin by writing a list of all the resentments they hold toward each other. Have the couple itemize each hurt or pain they recall in as much detail as possible. The couple is to write down exactly what happened and how they felt about it then and now.

One client shared the following list of resentments:

- "I feel hurt that you made sarcastic remarks about me in front of others."
- "I feel hurt that you found it hard to ever give me approval."
- "I resent that you wouldn't listen to me."

Another one of my clients shared:

- "I hate the fact that you called me trash and treated me the same."
- "I feel offended by the way you try to use me for your own benefit."
- "I resent your not loving me for who I am. You're always trying to change me into some unreal image."

Second, make the couple aware that they may experience emotional turmoil as they make their lists. Many have shared that as they face the resentments they hold toward their spouse, other old, buried feelings and experiences from childhood come to mind. They may find that they need to repeat this exercise for others in their past.

Third, encourage them to ask God to reveal to them their deep, hidden pools of memory so that their inner resentment can be flushed out. Also encourage them to thank God for letting it be alright to wade through and expel their feelings. I say to counselees, "Visualize Jesus Christ in the room with you, smiling and giving His approval to what you are doing." Imagine Him saying to you, "I want you to be cleansed and free. You no longer need to be emotionally crippled because of what happened to you."

Finally, after they have thoroughly verbalized their resentments in writing, ask them to spend time formulating how they will share their list with their spouse. Reading the list aloud is one way of formulating their thoughts. Then they are to select an appropriate time to discuss the list with their spouse. It is vital for them to share with their spouse requests for future improvement. It's always important for them to point toward their desired positive behaviors.[4]

Share Resentment with an Imaginary Person

For some people it is too difficult to share a list of resentments with their spouse. However, these people can and should still share. They can employ an intermediate approach of sharing their lists when their spouse is not present, which is practiced and recommended by many therapists.[5]

My instructions to each spouse are to prepare a quiet, comfortable room with two chairs facing each other. Separately they are to spend a few moments in prayer asking for the guidance of the Holy Spirit and the presence of Jesus Christ. Then they are to imagine Jesus coming into the room, walking up to them with a smile, telling them that He loves them and wanting them to be free from their resentments. Jesus encourages them to proceed.

Next, instruct each spouse to sit down in one of the chairs and imagine that their spouse is sitting in the other chair. They are to begin reading their list to the other chair as if their spouse were present. As they read, they are to imagine that their spouse thoughtfully accepts what is verbally shared by listening, nodding in acceptance and understanding their feelings.

At first each spouse may feel awkward and even embarrassed about reading to an empty chair, but these feelings will pass. As they read aloud, they may even find themselves expanding on what they had written. They may become very intense, angry, depressed or anxious as they rehearse these details aloud. Be sure to tell the spouses to verbalize these feelings in as much detail as possible. Remember, not only is the nonpresent spouse giving them permission to share all of their feelings, but Jesus Christ is also there encouraging them to release their inner resentment.

They may also find that talking through only one topic of resentment will be enough to handle in one sitting. If each spouse finds themselves becoming emotionally drained, then tell them to stop, rest and relax. They can resume the normal tasks of the day and come back to their list of resentments at another time, when they are fresh and composed.

Finally, before concluding each time of sharing, ask each spouse to close their eyes and visualize themselves, their spouse and Jesus standing together with their arms around one another's shoulders. They should spend several minutes visualizing this scene. They may wish to imagine the resented person verbally accepting what they have said. This is important, since one or both spouses may not accept what was said and could instead become angry. However, each spouse's reaction is not the purpose behind this exercise. What is important is that each spouse takes these steps to release their resentment.

Write a Letter to Release Resentment

Another helpful method for releasing resentment is to write a letter to the offending person. However, this letter is never to be delivered. It is a tool for the person to express resentful feelings in a more personal and detailed fashion than a list.

The letter should start with a salutation like any other letter. But in this letter they need not concern themselves with style, neatness or proper grammar and punctuation. Instead, concentrate on identifying, releasing and expressing feelings on paper in great detail.

A spouse may find it difficult to start. I often say, "Let out all the bad feelings that have been churning inside you. Don't stop to evaluate whether the feelings you express are good or bad, right or wrong. The feelings are there and need to be expressed. If you find the process emotionally exhausting you may want to complete it in stages over several days."

I ask many of my clients in therapy to write such a letter at home and bring it to their next session. Often they hand me the letter as they enter the room. "No," I say, "I'd like you to keep the letter and we will use it later." At the appropriate time I ask them to read the letter aloud to an empty chair in the room, imagining that the resented person is there listening.

I recall one client who wrote an extensive letter to her mother. She was surprised when I asked her to read it in my presence. During the first 15 minutes of reading, my client was very broken and tearful. But through the last five minutes, her weeping ceased and a positive, bright lilt to her voice concluded the letter. Some painful issues from her past were successfully dealt with through the exercise of writing and reading a letter.

Not only is it important to express and give up feelings of resentment, but it is also essential for the person to project a positive response to the person who has wronged them. Emptying the container of resentment is only half the battle. The other half is filling the container back up with feelings and expressions of love, acceptance, forgiveness and friendship.

Refocus on Spouse's Positive Qualities

Many of my clients have stated that they have neither positive nor negative feelings toward certain individuals. They are blasé. But what they have really developed is a state of emotional insulation toward those people, and insulation usually means an emotional blockage of some sort. This can occur as the person begins refocusing upon his or her spouse's positive qualities and potential. Remember to tell the counselee that forgiveness is a process and will take time, but ending resentment is the beginning of a new life.

Write Forgiveness Letter to Spouse

In the counseling office, I use an additional written exercise to help couples develop a positive response to resentment. Through this exercise, couples find and then eliminate any leftover feelings of resentment. I ask each spouse to take a blank sheet of paper and write their spouse's full name (or the name of the resented person) at the top. Below the name they are to write a "Dear (fill in the blank)" salutation.

Under the salutation each spouse should write "I forgive you for . . . " and then complete the sentence by writing down everything that has bothered them over the years. For example, someone may write, "I forgive you for always trying to control my life."

Next, each spouse needs to stop to capture the immediate thought that comes to mind after writing the statement of forgiveness. Does the thought contradict the concept of forgiveness they just expressed? Do they feel an inner rebuttal or protest of some kind? Is there any anger, doubt or caustic feeling that runs against their desire to forgive? All of these contradictory thoughts should be written immediately below their "I forgive you for . . . " statement. Tell them not to be surprised if their thoughts are so firm or vehement that it seems like they have not done any forgiving at all. The exercise continues by them writing "I forgive you for . . . " statements, followed by their immediate thoughts, even if they are contradictory.

Each spouse needs to keep repeating the process until they have drained all the pockets of resistance and resentment. They will know they have reached that point when they can think of no more contradictions or resentful responses to the statement of forgiveness they have written. Some people finish this exercise with only a few contradictory responses. Others have a great deal of resentment and use several pages to record their feelings. The following is a typical example of how a husband forgave his wife for her coldness toward him and her extramarital affair. Notice how his protest and contradictions to forgiveness become progressively less intense. Eventually, his resentment drains away to a point where he can finally say "I forgive you" and feel no further need for rebuttal.

Dear Liz, I forgive you for the way you've treated me over the years and for your unfaithfulness.
I'm just saying that. I can't forgive you right now. I'm so hurt.

Dear Liz, I forgive you for . . .
How do I know I can trust you after what you did?

Dear Liz, I forgive you for . . .
How do I know you're going to be any different? I can't take your coldness anymore.

Dear Liz, I forgive you for . . .
I'm really hesitant to open myself up to you anymore.

Dear Liz, I forgive you for . . .
I do love you, but I've been rejected so much. I'm afraid of being rejected again.

Dear Liz, I forgive you for . . .
I would like to forgive you at times. I don't like these feelings I have.

Dear Liz, I forgive you for . . .
*It's a bit better as I write this. I feel a bit funny and awkward as
I do this.*

Dear Liz, I forgive you for . . .
I wish this had never happened.

Dear Liz, I forgive you for . . .
*I know I've blamed you, and I feel you're responsible. But
maybe I contributed to the problems in some way.*

Dear Liz, I forgive you for . . .
My anger is less and maybe someday it will go away.

Three days after writing this letter to Liz, Jim repeated the exercise. In his second letter, after writing eight contradictory thoughts, Jim was able to conclude with several "I forgive you for . . . " statements with no rebuttals.

After each couple completes their own version of this exercise, I suggest the person sit opposite an empty chair, as described earlier, and follow these instructions: Visualize the resented person sitting in the empty chair verbally accepting your forgiveness. Take as long as you need for this step because it is very important. When you have finished the exercise, destroy your list of statements without showing it to anyone, as a symbol that, "Old things have passed away; behold, all things have become new" (2 Cor. 5:17, *KJV*).

And just like this verse, my hope is that you will soon be on your way to helping couples effectively, in six sessions or less, eliminate defeating patterns of behavior and thought, and move forward into what God intended for a marriage relationship—miraculous gifts like joy and peace.

EPILOGUE

If you have a desire to become more proficient in counseling and believe counseling is one of your gifts, many resources are available to you that enable growth. For instance, joining the American Association of Christian Counselors (AACC) and taking advantage of their resources and training conferences will assist you. Additionally, reading books and verbatim counseling sessions and viewing videos of actual counseling sessions will benefit you. Taking additional course work or working toward a doctorate of ministry in marriage and family counseling is another option. To contact the American Association of Christian Counselors, write: AACC, 1639 Rustic Village, Forest, VA 24551 or call 1-800-526-8673.

I also want to highlight some very helpful resources mentioned throughout the book. One resource is my own inventory, *The Marriage Checkup Questionnaire*, while the other resources are from different counselors and therapists.

1. *The Marriage Checkup Questionnaire* is published by Regal Books, 2300 Knoll Drive, Ventura, CA 93003. It is also available from Christian Marriage Enrichment, P.O. Box 2468, Orange, CA 92859. Remember that each spouse needs their own copy of the questionnaire, so they can reflect and respond privately to the inventory before discussing it with their spouse.
2. Should you encounter a couple in a state of crisis, your goal is to help them regain some sense of balance and stability. For more information, please refer to my book *Crisis Counseling*, which is also published by Regal Books.

3. Discussed in chapter 7, Dr. Willard Harley's book *His Needs, Her Needs* provides a practical "Man's Marital Needs Questionnaire" and a "Woman's Marital Needs Questionnaire," which may be helpful for you to use both in counseling and in marriage enrichment classes.

4. Many books and articles describing the multitude of behavioral approaches discussed in chapter 7 are available. Please refer to the endnotes for the titles and publishing information of these books.

5. To learn more about gender differences as mentioned in chapter 8, refer to Dr. John Gray's *Men Are from Mars and Women Are from Venus* (HarperCollins, 1993) and Dr. John Gottman's *Why Marriages Succeed or Fail* (Simon and Schuster, 1994).

I would also like to leave you with my thoughts on what you should do if you encounter a couple planning to divorce. You can take several approaches.

In the case of an individual or couple considering divorce, you want them to be fully cognizant of the ramifications of this step (which many are not).

Do not take an immediate approach of attempting to talk the couple or person out of this direction, as often they are already in a defensive stance and your response could intensify this. Instead, discuss what has led them to this point and what solutions they have tried. Then in a tentative manner and a caring tone of voice, ask if they believe they have taken every step possible to build their marriage, so they could say they've given it 150 percent effort. Some may say yes. If so, ask if you could suggest some possible options for reconciliation. If they say they're not sure, suggest that you and they commit to three months of counseling; and if at the end of that time no improvement has taken place, at least they can say they did put forth sufficient effort.

However, in order to accomplish this, I request the following:

1. Neither spouse mentions or threatens divorce to their spouse.
2. They each listen to the *Love Life* tapes by Dr. Ed Wheat and watch the video series *Before You Divorce*. I know of several churches who have encouraged couples in the midst of divorce proceedings to watch these tapes. As a result many of the couples brought the divorce proceedings to a halt, began working on their relationship and restored their marriage. It is possible for marriages to experience healing. For information regarding the tapes contact: Christian Marriage Enrichment, P.O. Box 2468, Orange, CA 92859 or call 1-800-875-7560.
3. The couple is requested to go on one field trip that involves visiting a divorce recovery workshop or meeting to simply listen to the stories of those going through the process. The hope is that by doing this, the couple's awareness is heightened about the divorce process, eventually leading them to reconsider moving back toward working out their differences. This suggestion may generate some discomfort, but who ever said counseling is comfortable and painless?

Finally, I would like to share with you a great way to help enrich the marriages of the couples in your church, as well as a way to lessen your counseling hours. This way is often found when pastors offer marriage enrichment classes in their church-es. If you implement a class at your church, some resources avail-able for your teaching use are my book *Communication: Key to Your Marriage* and the curriculum *How to Speak Your Spouse's Language*. This material can be taught not only in marriage sem-inars but also in Sunday School classes, retreats, small groups, etc. The curriculum contains a structured, outlined, time-sequenced format with learning activities, as well as many trans-parencies that you can use while teaching. You can order these materials from Christian Marriage Enrichment.

Remember, these are only a few resources at your disposal. It is important that as a counselor you explore the many options available to you and always continue to learn innovative meth-ods and approaches.

ENDNOTES

Chapter 1

1. DeLoss D. Friesen, Ph.D., and Ruby M. Friesen, Ph.D., *Counseling and Marriage* (Dallas: Word, Inc., 1989), p. 41.
2. Ibid., p. 42.
3. Ibid.
4. Everett L. Worthington, Jr., *Marriage Counseling* (Downers Grove, IL: InterVarsity Press, 1989), pp. 161-162.
5. Ibid.
6. Gary Oliver, Ph.D., Monte Hasng, Psy.D., and Matthew Richburg, M.A., *Promoting Change Through Brief Therapy in Christian Counseling* (Wheaton, IL: Tyndale House, 1997), pp. 78-89.
7. H. Norman Wright, *The Marriage Checkup Questionnaire* (Ventura, CA: Regal Books, 2002).

Chapter 2

1. Lois Madow, *The Snare* (Colorado Springs, CO: NavPress, 1988).

Chapter 3

1. Otto Kroeger and Janet M. Thuesen, *Type Talk* (New York: Bantam Books, 1988).
2. Ibid., pp. 17-18.
3. H. Norman Wright, *Communication: Key to Your Marriage* (Ventura, CA: Regal Books, 2000), pp. 147-183.
4. Robert Dilts, *Applications of Neuro-Linguistic Programming* (Cupertino, CA: Meta Publications, 1983).

Chapter 4

1. Dr. John Gottman, *Why Marriages Succeed or Fail* (New York: Simon and Schuster, 1994), p. 57.
2. Ibid., pp. 59-61.
3. John L. Walter and Jane E. Peller, *Becoming Solution-Focused in Brief Therapy* (New York: Brunner/Mazel Inc., 1992), pp. 2-6.
4. David Dillon, Ph.D., *Short-Term Counseling* (Dallas: Word, Inc., 1991), pp. 123-124.
5. Walter and Peller, *Becoming Solution-Focused in Brief Therapy*, pp. 96-98.
6. Dillon, *Short-Term Counseling*, pp. 92-93.
7. Walter and Peller, *Becoming Solution-Focused in Brief Therapy*, pp. 52-59.
8. Ibid., pp. 79-81.

9. Ibid., pp. 90-93.
10. Michele Weiner-Davis, *Divorce Busting* (New York: Summit Books, 1992), p. 128.
11. Ibid., pp. 124-140.
12. S. de Shazer, *Clues: Investigating Solutions in Brief Therapy* (New York: W. W. Norton and Co., 1988), p. 184.
13. Darryl Gates, *Chief* (New York: Bantam Books, 1992), pp. 67-68.

Chapter 5

1. Richard B. Stuart, *Helping Couples Change: A Social Learning Approach to Marital Therapy* (New York: The Guilford Press, 1980), pp. 198-199, 201-202.
2. Richard B. Stuart, "An Operant Interpersonal Program for Couples," in *Treating Relationships* (Lake Mills, IA: Graphic Publishing Co., 1976), pp. 124-125.
3. Gregory W. Lester, Ernst Beckham and Donald H. Baucom, "Implementation of Behavioral Marital Therapy," *Journal of Marital and Family Therapy*, American Association for Marriage and Family Therapy 6, no. 2 (April 1980), pp. 191-194.

Chapter 6

1. Joseph Strayhorn, M.D., "Social-Exchange Theory: Cognitive Restructuring in Marital Therapy," *Family Process* 17 (December 1978), p. 446.
2. H. Norman Wright, *The Marriage Checkup Questionnaire* (Ventura, CA: Regal Books, 2002).
3. Everett L. Worthington, Jr., and Douglas McMurray, *Marriage Conflicts* (Grand Rapids, MI: Baker Books, 1994), pp. 117-118.
4. Ibid., pp. 119-120.
5. Ibid., pp. 117-122.

Chapter 7

1. Willard F. Harley, Jr., *His Needs, Her Needs* (Grand Rapids, MI: Fleming H. Revell, 1986), p. 10.
2. Ibid., p. 16.
3. Clifford Notarius, Ph.D., and Howard Markman, Ph.D., *We Can Work It Out* (New York: G. P. Putnam Publishing Group, 1993), pp. 28, 70-75.
4. Leonard Zunnin, *Contact: The First Four Minutes* (New York: Ballantine Books, 1972), p. 133ff.
5. H. Norman Wright, *The Pillars of Marriage* (Ventura, CA: Regal Books, 1979), pp. 74-75.
6. Willard F. Harley, Jr., *His Needs, Her Needs* (Grand Rapids, MI: Fleming H. Revell, 1986), n.p.

Chapter 8

1. *Webster's New World College Dictionary*, s.v. "conflict."
2. John Gottman, *Why Marriages Succeed or Fail* (New York: Simon and Schuster, 1994), p. 28.
3. Ibid., p. 158.
4. Clifford Notarius, Ph.D. and Howard Markman, Ph.D., *We Can Work It Out* (New York: G. P. Putnam Publishing Group, 1993), p. 44.
5. Bernard Callahanard, Jr., and Constance Callahanard, eds., *Handbook of Marriage Counseling* (Palo Alto, CA: Science and Behavior Books, Inc., 1976).
6. John Allan Lavender, *Your Marriage Needs Three Love Affairs* (Denver, CO: Accent Books, 1978), pp. 118-119.
7. *Minnesota Couples Communication Program Handbook* (Minneapolis, MN: Couples Communication Program, 1972), pp. 23-31.
8. H. Norman Wright, *Communication and Conflict Resolution in Marriage* (Elgin, IL: David C. Cook Publishers, 1977), p. 12.
9. John Strong, "A Marital Conflict Resolution Model Redefining Conflict to Achieve Intimacy," *Journal of Marriage and Family Counseling* (July 1975), pp. 269-276.
10. Notarius and Markman, *We Can Work It Out*, p. 218.
11. Ibid.

Chapter 9

1. Aaron T. Beck, *Love Is Never Enough* (New York: HarperCollins, 1988), p. 267.
2. Ibid.
3. Gayla Margolin, "Conjoint Marital Therapy to Enhance Anger Management and Reduce Spouse Abuse," *The American Journal of Family Therapy* 7, no. 2 (summer 1979), pp. 18-20.
4. Howard Halpern, *Cutting Loose: An Adult's Guide to Coming to Terms with Your Parents* (New York: Bantam Books, 1978), p. 212ff; Matthew L. Linn and Dennis Linn, *Healing of Memories* (Ramsey, NJ: Paulist Press, 1974), pp. 94-96; Matthew L. Linn and Dennis Linn, *Healing Life's Hurts* (Ramsey, NJ: Paulist Press, 1977), p. 218ff.
5. David L. Luecke, *The Relationship Manual* (Columbia, MD: Relationship Institute, 1981), pp. 88-91.